RAMBAN

COMMENTARY ON THE TORAH

פירוש הרמב״ן על התורה

BEREISHIS
PART I

—◦◉◦—

Selected portions of Nachmanides

Annotated and
Translated
by
Rabbi Avraham Yaakov Finkel

YESHIVATH BETH MOSHE
SCRANTON, PA.

CONTENTS

הקדמה
מראש הישיבה
מורינו הרב יעקב שניידמאן שליט"א

הבא ללמוד תנ"ך יהיה לו תועלת הרבה אם קודם לימודו יתבונן
בשתי נקודות. ראשונה, דיש מקום לטעות גדול בלימוד תנ"ך דמי
שבא ללמוד תורה שבע"פ ובפרט אם בא ללמוד גמרא יודע מיד
דהוא צריך לרב ומסורה איך ללמוד. וכמו שכתב הרמב"ם בהקדמתו
על משנה תורה וז"ל וכל אלו הגאונים שעמדו בארץ ישראל ובארץ
שנער ובספרד ובצרפת למדו דרך הגמרא והוציאו לאור תעלומותיו
וביארו ענינו, לפי שדרך עמוקה דרכו עד למאוד עכ"ל ובזמנינו אינו
מספיק מה שפירשו בדורות הראשונים, דהם פירשו לפי מדרגתם
ולפי מה שנתקשו בדורותם, ובדורותינו נתקשו מאד אפי' בדברים
שהיו פשוטים בעיניהם וצריכים אנו לרב אף בענינים שהיו דברים
פשוטים להם, וכל א' מכיר זה בקל. אבל מי שבא ללמוד תנ"ך, נראים
לו הדברים כמו שהם כתובים כדברים פשוטים, ונקל לחשוב לעצמו
דכיון שיודע השפה אינו נחוץ לו לרב או למסורה; איך ללומדה.
ובאמת זה טעות גדולה ומביא לידי מכשולות הרבה בעניני השקפה
ואמונה. אלא צריך להבין כי פירוש רש"י ואחריו הרמב"ן על התורה
הם כפירוש הראשונים על הגמ' אשר פשוט לכל דבלימוד גמ' מבל-
עדי פירושם א"א לזוז, וכמו כן בלימוד חומש א"א להתחיל בלא
פירוש רש"י ואם יש בידו צריך להמשיך בלימוד הרמב"ן שהם **פתחו**
פתח להבין בכל פרשה, ולעמוד על העינים הגדולים והסודות שיו-
צאים מכל פרשה ופרשה. וכמו שבלימוד גמ' פשוט דאנו צריכים
לרב ולמסורה להבין אף דברי הראשונים לאמיתם כמו כן בלימוד
חומש רש"י ורמב"ן, אחר הלימוד וההתבוננות בהם עדיין צריכים
לרב ומסורה לעמוד על מה שהם פתחו וגילו, דהרבה דברים אמרו
במעט תיבות, דזהו כח הראשונים לכתוב בקיצור ולכלול ענינים

v

הרבה בקיצורם. ומה שהישיבה הדפיס ענינים של הרמב״ן מפירושו
לחומש באנגלית אין כוונתנו שאדם ילמוד הרמב״ן ויחשוב שיכול
לגמור הלימוד בעצמו, רק כוונתנו להועיל בלימוד הרמב״ן כדי
שיכול אח״כ לגמור לימודו ע״י קשר עם רב, והועלנו ע״י התרגום
שלא יהיה דברי הרמב״ן כספר סתום דהרי ידוע דלשונו בקיצור וגם
כמה פעמים קשה לעמוד על כוונתו בדיוק.

שנית, לימוד חומש ורש״י הוא סיוע גדול לחזק אמונתנו. ואף
שאין דרך רש״י לבאר ענינים עפ״י מחקר ופילוסופיא, ולא יתחזק
אמונתנו עפ״י דרכי המדע מ״מ לימודו מועיל מאד. והטעם לפי מה
שקבלתי מרבותי הוא דאין עיקר כח אמונתנו ובפרט בדור שלנו בנוי
על דרכי השכל ועל כח המופת אלא שיש בנפשנו כמו ראייה נפשיית
להכיר שיש בורא עולם שברא העולם ומנהיגה. וביאור הענין הוא
שכל א׳ יש לו נשמה ממעל שרואה וע״י כח הראייה בנשמתו נקבע
ראייה זה באדם. ואף על פי כן צריך לחיזוק הרבה. דהרי מצבו
בעוה״ז פועל עליו להטעותו ולהסיח דעתו ממה שהוא ברור אצלו.
למשל מי שראה שיש סכנה בדרך ויודע דצריך ליזהר במהלכו מ״מ
בלא חיזוק הוא שוכח ואינה משים לב להיזהר ובא לידי סכנה. כמו
כן באמונתנו פשוט לנו בראייה נפשיית שיש בורא עולם ומ״מ צריך
לחיזוק תמידית שלא לשכוח ושלא להסיח דעת. ולימוד רש״י הוא
הסיוע גדולה לזה דדרכו בפירושו פועל על נפש האדם להחזיק
האמונה בלבו. ואחריו פירוש הרמב״ן שבנוי על פירוש רש״י ומבאר
ענינים גדולים ויסודיים כדי שיהא ברורים ביותר. ומי שלומד רש״י
ורמב״ן בטוח שיהיה לו חיזוק באמונתו, ועי״ז יזכה להיות מן הדבקים
להקב״ה כראוי.

SUMMARY OF
RABBI YAAKOV SCHNAIDMAN'S
PROLOGUE

———◄◉►———

One who wishes to study Scriptures must bear in mind two points. Firstly, when one studies work of the Oral Torah such as the Talmud, one realizes that he must have a teacher and depend on tradition, as the Rambam says, the path to understanding the Talmud is very deep; one must rely on the interpretations of the earlier Rabbis. In our times we cannot rely on the interpretations of the earlier Rabbis as the Rambam advised, because we find the subject much more difficult; things they took for granted we cannot understand. But unfortunately, many people when studying Scripture, think that as long as they understand the language, they can understand the text properly without being taught it. This is a grave error, which can cause fundamental mistakes in belief and outlook. Just as one cannot learn the Talmud without the help of the earlier commentators, so too one cannot approach the Written Torah without the help of Rashi and the Ramban, for they open our eyes to understand each Parsha explaining the hidden meaning of the text. And just as one cannot approach the Talmud without a teacher and guide, so too, one cannot rely on one's own understanding of the early commentators to Scripture without a teacher. By publishing the Ramban in English the yeshiva does not mean to imply that one can fully understand his words on his own. Rather

Rabbi Yaakov Schnaidman is the Rosh Yeshivah of Yeshivath Beth Moshe Scranton, Pennsylvania.

he can begin learning the difficult language of the Ramban on his own, eventually completing his study with a capable teacher.

Secondly, studying Rashi and the Ramban on the Torah strengthens one's faith. Although Rashi does not delve into philosophical and logical arguments and one's faith will not be strengthened rationally, studying his commentary will be of great benefit. I have been taught, that this is because our faith is not based on rational arguments; rather we have within our Divine soul the power to perceive the truth that this world has a Creator and Guide. This is especially true today. We must strengthen this inherent truth, for if we don't, the pleasures and allurement of this world will lead us astray. Learning Rashi and the Ramban's commentary on the Torah helps us in this regard, strengthening the faith in our hearts and helping to properly attach ourselves to Hashem.

TRANSLATOR'S INTRODUCTION

———=◉=———

R abbi Moshe ben Nachman (Nachmanides), better known as Ramban—the acronym of his Hebrew name—was one of the greatest Torah commentators. He also is acclaimed as an outstanding Talmudist and Kabbalist. Born in Gerona, Spain in 1194, he was a descendant of a renowned rabbinical family.

At the age of seventy-two, the Ramban settled in Eretz Yisrael. Finding Yerushalayim in utter desolation in the wake of the out rages of the marauding crusaders, he began to rebuild the devastated Jewish community. He wrote to his son in Spain, "Eretz Yisrael lies in ruin, and the holier the place the greater the destruction. The most desolate place of all is Yerushalayim." In all of Yerushalayim there were only two Jews, and not one *sefer Torah*. The Ramban converted a ruined old building into a synagogue, organized Jews to come back to Yerushalayim, and brought a *sefer Torah* all the way from Shechem.

The Ramban died in 1270 at the age of seventy-six. Strangely, the site of his grave is unknown. According to one version he is buried in Haifa alongside the tomb of R. Yechiel of Paris. According to another, his tomb is next to Me'aras Hamachpelah in Chevron. No matter which is correct, it is certainly true that the Ramban's resting place is in the minds and hearts of his countless students to whom his commentaries are part of Chumash and Talmud.

THE RAMBAN'S *PEIRUSH AL HATORAH*

T he Ramban's monumental commentary on the Torah is indispensable for a clear understanding of the Torah text.

In his Torah commentary the Ramban sometimes disagrees with Rashi's interpretations, and often inserts very concise Kabbalistic insights. In a few cryptic words he hides profound Kabbalistic concepts which he refers to as *sod* (secret, mystery). He usually closes his Kabbalistic comments with *vehamaskil yavin*, "those who know Kabbalah will understand." Rabbi Yitzchak Luria (the Ari), the great 16th century Kabbalist, praises the depth and reliability of the mystical portions of the Ramban's commentary.

There are many indications that the Ramban wrote his Torah commentary late in life. For example, in his commentary at the end of *sefer Shemos* he says: "Thus is completed the Book of Redemption, . . . And blessed be G-d who has helped me come thus far [to Eretz Yisrael], who renews His servant's youth in his old age, who satisfies his hunger with Torah."

AN INSPIRING INSIGHT

In conclusion I wish to quote the Ramban's inspiring commentary on the verse, *I will make the Land desolate that even your enemies who live there will be astonished* (Vayikra 26:32).

Says the Ramban: This is a hopeful message, assuring us us that throughout all our exiles, our Land will not accept our enemies. It also offers great proof and holds a promise for us, for in the whole inhabited part of the world there is not such a good and spacious land which was always settled, and yet is as ruined as Eretz Yisrael is today. For ever since we left it, it has not accepted any nation or people, although they all try to colonize it, they all failed.

The present volume contains a wide-ranging selection of the Ramban's commentaries on the first thirty chapters of Sefer Bereishis (parashas Bereishis—Vayeitzei). I have used the authoritative and annotated edition of Mossad Harav Kook (Yerushalayim, 1967). It is my hope that that this translation of Peirush Haramban will give the reader a deeper understanding of the Torah text and an appreciation of the towering wisdom and sublime character of the Ramban.

AVRAHAM YAAKOV FINKEL
Tamuz, 5764/2004

RAMBAN – *NACHMANIDES*
COMMENTARY ON THE TORAH
פירוש הרמב״ן על התורה

BEREISHIS

PART I

הקדמה
INTRODUCTION

——◆——

WHEN DID MOSHE WRITE THE TORAH?

O ur teacher Moshe wrote the book of *Bereishis* together with the whole Torah, as dictated to him by the Holy One, blessed be He.

He probably wrote it on Mount Sinai, where he was told, *Come up to Me, to the mountain, and remain there. I will give you the stone tablets, the Torah and the commandments that I have written for [the people's] instruction* (*Shemos* 24:12). *The stone tablets* refers to the tablets which were [engraved with] the Ten Commandments. *The commandments* refers to both the—positive and negative mitzvos. Hence, *the Torah* [which means the teaching] must mean the stories from the beginning of *Bereishis,* which teach people how [to live] faithfully.

When Moshe descended the mountain,[1] he wrote the Torah from the beginning of *Bereishis* until the end of the section dealing with the building of the *Mishkan* (Tabernacle). He wrote the rest of the Torah at the end of the fortieth year [of the wandering in the wilderness] when he said [to the Levites], *Take this scroll and place it to the side of the ark of Hashem your G-d's covenant* (*Devarim* 31:26).

---

1   After bringing down the second Tablets, on the day after Yom Kippur.

I base this on the opinion [of R. Yochanan] who says[2] that the
Torah was written one section at a time. [As each section was transmitted to Moshe, he wrote it down, joining all the sections together at the end]. However, according to [R. Shimon b. Lakish]
who says that the Torah was given as one complete unit,[3] everything was written in the fortieth year when Moshe was told, *Now
write for yourselves this song and teach it to b'nei Yisrael, so that it becomes fluent in their mouths* (*Devarim* 31:19). He then told [the
Levites], *Take this scroll and place it to the side of the ark of the
covenant of Hashem your G-d* (*Devarim* 31:26).

MOSHE WROTE IN THE THIRD PERSON

In either case, [whether the Torah was written in sections or as
one unit,] it would seem proper for Moshe to begin *Bereishis*
with the words, "G-d spoke to Moshe all these words, saying." But
it was written without specifying [the author] because Moshe did
not write the Torah [in first person], as the prophets, who noted
themselves [as authors] did. For example, Yechezkel often says, *The
word of Hashem came to me, saying, "Son of Man,"* (*Yechezkel*
3:16,17), and Yirmeyah says, *The word of Hashem came to me*
(*Yirmeyah* 1:4). However Moshe wrote the history of the early
generations, and his own ancestry, history, and events, in the third
person, even saying, *G-d spoke to Moshe and said to him* (*Shemos*
6:2), as if he were speaking about another person. Thus, Moshe is
not mentioned in the Torah until his birth, and even then he is
mentioned as if someone else were speaking about him.

It is not contradictory to find Moshe speaking about himself [in
the first person,] in *sefer Devarim* saying, *At that time I pleaded
with Hashem* (*Devarim* 3:23) and, *I prayed to Hashem* (9:26), because *sefer Devarim* begins with the words, *These are the words that*

---

[2]   *Gittin* 60a.
[3]   Though the sections were given to Moshe orally from time to time, he wrote
them all down at the end of the forty years of wandering (*Gittin* 61a).

Moshe spoke to all Yisrael (*Devarim* 1:1). Thus *Devarim* is a direct quote of Moshe's speeches.

THE TORAH EXISTED BEFORE CREATION

The Torah is written in third person because it existed before the creation of the world, and needless to say, before the birth of Moshe Rabbeinu, as our tradition teaches that the Torah was written [before creation] with letters of black fire on a background of white fire.[4] Moshe acted as a scribe who copies from an ancient book; therefore he wrote it in third person[5]. Certainly Moshe heard the entire Torah—from the first word in *Bereishis* until the final words of the Torah, *before the eyes of all Yisrael*—from the mouth of G-d, [just as Baruch ben Neriah, Yirmeyah's scribe, wrote *Megillas Eichah* as he heard it from his master,] as he says, *From his own mouth he would dictate all these words, and I would write on the book with ink* (*Yirmeyah* 36:18).

G-d told Moshe about the creation of all things, in the world above and below. He also advised Moshe about [the mystical] workings of the Divine Chariot,[6] which the prophets describe, the process of Creation, and everything which has been transmitted orally to the Sages. Moshe also learned about the four elements of nature: the inanimate, the vegetative, the moving animals, and man's living soul. He was taught about the creation, essence, powers, functions, and mortality of all these things. This was all written in the Torah, either explicitly or implicitly.

---

4   Rashi on *Devarim* 33:2.
5   Unlike prophecies to the other prophets where they were given a specific message at that time. The Torah is timeless and existed without Moshe Rabbeinu.
6   As described in *Yechezkel* 1.

THE FIFTY GATES OF UNDERSTANDING

Our Sages said: Fifty gates of understanding were created, and all but one were given to Moshe, as it says, *You have made him little less than G-d* (*Tehillim* 8:6). The Sages mean there are fifty kinds of understanding in the creation of the world. One level of understanding relates to the creation of inanimate minerals, another level of understanding relates to the creation of vegetation, yet another relates to the creation of trees, another to animals, another to birds, another to creeping things, and another to fish. [Having mastered these gates of understanding, one] is able to understand the creation of man, intuiting the essence of the human soul and its power to exert influence on the heavenly realm [through prayer and good deeds]. From there he can attain the spiritual level described by the Sages as follows:[7] "If a person stole, [the holy man on this spiritual level] knows it; if a person committed adultery, [the holy man] recognizes it; if a person is suspected of having intercourse with a woman in her *niddah* state, [the holy man] is cognizant of it. Above all, he is aware if someone engages in witchcraft. From that lofty level of understanding he advances to an understanding of the heavenly spheres, stars and planets. There is a different branch of wisdom for each of these fields of knowledge. Tradition has it that there are forty-nine gates of understanding. It is possible that the fiftieth gate, which has not been revealed to any human being, deals with the knowledge of the Creator.

Don't let the saying "fifty gates were created" mislead you [into thinking that the fiftieth gate which deals with the essence of Hashem is also a creation. The word created] refers only to the majority, for the fiftieth gate was never created. The number 50 is clearly alluded to in the Torah in connection with the counting of the *omer* [*You shall count fifty days* (*Vayikra* 23:16)] and the *yovel* [*You shall sanctify the fiftieth year* (*Vayikra* 25:10)], whose secrets I will reveal when I reach that point, G-d willing.

---

[7]   *Heichalos Rabbasi* 1:3.

PROFOUND WISDOM IN EVERY LETTER OF THE TORAH

The knowledge transmitted to Moshe through the gates of wisdom was written in the Torah explicitly, or in allusions through words or through numerical values of words. [It was also alluded to] through the form of the letters, some written normally, some changed in form, with bent or crooked letters and other aberrations, or through the tips of letters or the [small decorative] crowns.

[In this connection] the Sages said: When Moshe ascended on high, he found the Holy One, blessed be He, adding crowns to certain letters of the Torah. Asked Moshe, "What is the purpose of these [little crowns]?" Replied G-d, "Many generations from now a man named [Rabbi] Akiva ben Yosef will extract piles and piles of laws [from each of these crowns." Requested Moshe, "Please allow me to see this man." Replied G-d, "Step back." Moshe sat in the eighth row in the beis midrash of R. Akiva. When he did not understand the laws being taught he was disheartened until the students asked R. Akiva,] "From where do you know this?" R. Akiva replied, "It is a law given to Moshe on Sinai." [When Moshe heard himself being quoted, he was reassured.] Indeed these allusions cannot be understood except through explanations handed down through oral tradition from master to disciple, back to Moshe Rabbeinu.

Referring to this, the Sages said, King Chizkiah [received a visit from envoys of the king of Babylonia and]: "He showed them the Book of Crowns." This is a popular book, readily available[8] which explains which letters in the Torah have little crowns. The Sages accorded this book much praise, not for the little crowns, but for the many profound secrets in its commentaries. It was these secrets that King Chizkiah divulged.

Furthermore, in Midrash Shir Hashirim Rabbah 1:29, the Sages explain: It says, *He announced to you His covenant* (*Devarim* 4:13),

---

8   Paris, 1869; Nuremberg, 1923.

meaning, *He announced to you* the Book of *Bereishis*, which relates the beginning of G-d's creation of the world.[9] [The verse continues,] *instructing you to keep the Ten Commandments*—ten for the Written Torah and ten for the Talmud [i.e., the Oral Torah which is the interpretation of the Written Torah]. For [if the Oral Torah was not given on Sinai,] from what source did Elihu ben Barachel the Buzite reveal to Yisrael the secrets of the Behemoth and the Leviathan? And from what source did Yechezkel reveal the mystical order of the Divine Chariot? Thus Shlomoh wrote, *The King brought me into His chamber* (*Shir Hashirim* 1:4) meaning that all knowledge can be found in the Torah.

THE TORAH IS THE SOURCE OF SHLOMOH'S WISDOM

King Shlomoh to whom G-d gave wisdom and insight, derived his knowledge from the Torah. From it he learned the secret of all things created, even the secrets of the healing qualities of plants, enabling him to write a book about herbal medicine. For it says, *He spoke of the trees from the cedar which is in the Lebanon, down to the hyssop which grows out of the wall* (1 *Melachim* 5:13).

I have seen in the Aramaic translation of the book called "The Great Wisdom of Shlomoh" [that Shlomoh wrote:] "Whether king or commoner, we all enter the world the same way [at birth], and we leave the world the same way [in death]. Therefore, I have prayed for wisdom, and my prayer was answered; I called out to G-d, and knowledge was granted me. I valued it more than the scepter and the throne."

He also wrote: "It is G-d who grants knowledge that contains no falsehood, so one can know how the world came into being, the formation of the constellations, the weather of the changing seasons, the fixed positions of the stars, the docile nature of cattle, the

---

9   The Hebrew word for covenant and creation are similar.

savage temper of wild beasts, the power of the wind, the thoughts of man, the relationship of trees, and the strength of roots; everything hidden and everything revealed I know." Shlomoh knew all this from the Torah; learning everything from its plain meaning, its derivations, its letters and its small crowns, as I have mentioned above.

And so we find, *Shlomoh's wisdom surpassed the wisdom of all the people of the east* (1 *Melachim* 5:10). He surpassed them even in divination and black magic which were their specialties, as it says, *Because they were filled with sorceries of the East and divinations like the Philistines* (*Yeshayah* 2:6). The Sages said further: What was the wisdom of the people of the east? They knew the secret language of the birds. *Shlomoh's wisdom surpassed . . . all the wisdom of Egypt* (1 *Melachim* 5:10) teaches that he surpassed the Egyptians in sorcery which is the wisdom of Egypt, and in the knowledge of how to grow plants. We know from the Book of Egyptian Agriculture that the Egyptians were very advanced in the technique of planting crops and grafting different species.

In this vein, the Sages said: Shlomoh planted peppers in Eretz Yisrael. How was he able to plant them? Shlomoh was a wise man, who knew the basic composition of the world. How [did this help him in planting crops]? It says, *Out of Zion, perfect in beauty, G-d appeared* (*Tehillim* 50:2). Out of Zion the whole world was created. And we are taught: [There was a certain stone in the Holy of Holies called *Shesiah—"Foundation Stone"* on which the Ark rested.] Why was it called "Foundation Stone"? Because from this central point the entire world was formed.[10] Shlomoh knew which of the world's arteries extends [from Zion] to Ethiopia, and on it he planted peppers, which produced fruits immediately, as he said, *And I planted trees, bearing all kinds of fruit* (*Koheles* 2:5).

---

[10] *Yoma* 54b. The idea is, that Zion was created first, and around it other clods of matter, formations, and continents were added until the earth was completed.

The Whole Torah Comprises the Names of *Hakadosh Baruch Hu*

We have a mystic tradition that the whole Torah is comprised of names of the Holy One, blessed be He, and that the letters [of the Torah] can be broken up differently to form Divine names. For example: the letters of the verse *bereishis bara elokim* can be divided to form the words: *berosh yisbarei Elokim*. Similarly, the entire Torah [can be divided into any number of different words]. In addition there are other forms of counting the combinations and numerical equivalents which allude to the holy Names. *Rashi* explains in his commentary on the Gemara[11] how the Great Divine Name of seventy-two letters is contained in the three verses [beginning with the words] *vayisa* "he went" (*Shemos* 14:19), *vayavo* "he came" (14:20), and *vayeit* "he stretched out" (14:21).

Since the entire Torah is comprised of Divine Names, a *sefer Torah* with even one letter added or deleted is unfit for use, even if the meaning remains unchanged. For example, this law applies to the word *osam*, which occurs with a *vav* 39 times—[and more often without a *vav*]. Neither type may be changed. The same applies to similar cases. Although it seems to make no difference in our understanding of the subject, [the Torah becomes unfit because the missing or additional letters change the Divine Names].

The gravity of this matter prompted the Torah scholars to count all the words in the Torah that are written either full or incomplete; and to write books spelling out the Masoretic text of the Torah, going back to Ezra the Scribe and prophet who worked on this. The Sages derived this rule from the verse, *They read in the scroll of G-d's Torah, clearly, with the application of wisdom, and they helped [the people] understand the reading*" (*Nechemiah* 8:8). [The Gemara in *Nedarim 37b* expounds: *with the application of wisdom*—refers to the division of sentences; *understand the reading*—refers to the accentuation (*trop*); others say: to the *masoros*.[12]]

---

11   *Sukkah* 45a, s.v. *ani.*
12   i.e., the full and defective readings (*malei* and *chaseir*).

It seems that the Torah, [written before creation] with letters of black fire on a background of white fire was written as an uninterrupted string of letters. Without spaces between words it could be read as mystical Divine names and also the way we read it, making the Torah and the mitzvos understandable. Moshe was given the Torah with the words spaced apart to teach the mitzvos, whereas the way to read the Divine names was transmitted to him orally. The masters of Kabbalah write the letters of the Great Name [of 72 letters] in a contiguous fashion, and then split it into words of three or more letters.

THE RAMBAN EXPLAINS WHY HE WROTE HIS COMMENTARY

At this point I shall answer those who asked me why I wrote a commentary on the Torah. I want to follow the example of the early rabbis, bringing spiritual fulfillment to the students, who though wearied from the troubles of the exile, read the weekly *parashah* on Shabbos and Yom Tov. I hope to draw their hearts with the plain interpretation of the Torah text, and include insights that appeal to students and masters of Kabbalah. May the gracious G-d favor and bless us, and may we find grace and good understanding in the eyes of G-d and man.

A WORD OF CAUTION

Let me caution the reader to avoid delving into the mystical and Kabbalistic commentaries in this book. No matter how hard he tries, he will not understand my remarks unless he is guided by a learned Kabbalist. [For a layman] to ponder these matters is foolish, useless, and harmful. His reasoning will bring evil, as if he spoke maliciously against G-d, which is unforgivable. As it says, *A person who wanders from the intelligent way will rest in the congre-*

gation of the dead (*Mishlei* 21:16), and, *They must not cross the boundary in order to see the Divine* (*Shemos* 19:21), and, *For Hashem, our G-d is like a consuming fire, a jealous G-d* (*Devarim* 4:24). G-d will show the wonders of the Torah to those He favors.

May those who study our commentary find novel insights on the plain meaning of the Torah and the *Midrashim*. Let them be warned from our holy Rabbis, who said:" Do not probe into things beyond your grasp; do not research things stronger than you, do not seek to learn things hidden from you, do not question things concealed from you. Reflect on things permitted to you, but do not concern yourself with mysticism."[13]

---

[13] *Bereishis Rabbah* 8:2.

בראשית

BEREISHIS

———◦◉◦———

THE B'NAI YISRAEL'S CLAIM TO ERETZ YISRAEL

1:1 In the beginning, G-d created the heaven and the earth.

In the beginning—Rabbi Yitzchak said: The Torah [which is a book of laws] should have begun with the verse, *This month shall be for you the first of the months* (*Shemos* 12:2), since this is the first mitzvah given to Yisrael. Why does it start with the Creation? So that if the nations of the world say to Yisrael, "You are robbers, because you have seized the lands of the seven Canaanite nations," Yisrael can answer, "The whole world belongs to the Holy One, blessed be He. He created it and gave it to whom He pleased, He gave it to them and He took the land from them and gave it to us." This aggada is quoted by Rashi.

One may argue that indeed it was necessary to begin the Torah with the verse, *In the beginning G-d created,* since this is the foundation of our faith, and whoever does not believe this, denies a fundamental principle of our faith and has no Torah at all.

[The answer is] that the story of Creation is a deep mystery which cannot be understood from the verses [alone]. It can only be understood through the [mystical] tradition handed down through the generations from Moshe Rabbeinu who received it from the mouth of the Al-mighty. Those who know the mystery must hide it. Therefore Rabbi Yitzchak said it was not necessary to start the Torah with

In the beginning G-d created and relate: the creation of the first day, the second day, and the other days; the lengthy account of the creation of Adam and Chavah, their transgression and punishment, and the story of Gan Eden and Adam's expulsion, because these cannot be fully understood from the Torah text. Surely there is no need to record the generations of the Flood and Dispersion. People who believe in the Torah would believe in Creation without these [lengthy] chapters. [It would suffice to say,] *It was during the six weekdays that Hashem made the heaven, the earth, the sea, and all that is in them, and He rested on the seventh day* (*Shemos* 20:11), as mentioned in the Ten Commandments. The details of Creation could have been transmitted orally to chosen individuals as a tradition going back to Moshe who received it on Sinai along with the Oral Torah.

Rabbi Yitzchak answers: the Torah starts with *In the beginning G-d created* and discusses the Creation, the creation of man, how G-d made him master over all the world, and how *Gan Eden,* the best place on earth, was his residence until he was driven out because of his sin. [The Torah relates] how the people of the generation of the Flood were eliminated from the face of the earth because of their iniquity, and only the righteous [Noach] and his sons were saved. [The Torah relates,] how the sin of the generation of the Dispersion caused them to be scattered to the four corners of the earth where they settled and branched out into families and nations with different languages.

The Torah thus teaches us that whenever a nation continually sins, it loses its land and another people takes over its territory, for this has been the law of G-d from day one. [Surely the people of Canaan deserved this fate, for in addition to their sins,] Canaan was cursed and sold as a servant forever (*Bereishis* 9:25-27). It would not be right for Canaan to live in the best place in the entire world. Instead, the servants of G-d—the descendants of Avraham who loved Him—should possess it. And so it says, *He gave them [the Jews] the lands of nations; they took possession of the wealth of peoples, that they might keep His laws and observe His teachings* (*Tehillim* 105:44,45). This means that, G-d drove those who rebelled against Him from Eretz Yisrael, while the ones who serve Him settled there instead. Only by serving G-d have we inherited the Land, and if we sin against Him, the Land will vomit us out, just as it vomited out the nation that was there before us.

The full text of above-mentioned commentary by Rashi is found in *Bereishis Rabbah* 1:3 where it says: Rabbi Yehoshua of Sachnin opened his lecture quoting the verse, *The strength of His deeds He declared to His people* (*Tehillim* 11:6). Why did the Holy One, blessed be He, reveal to Yisrael what was created on the first and second day? It is to preclude the seven nations [who inhabited Eretz Yisrael] from taunting Yisrael, saying: "You are nothing but a nation of robbers!" To which Yisrael retorts: "And you, aren't your hands filled with loot? *Did not the Kaftorim who came from Kaftor defeat [the Avvim] occupying their territory* (*Devarim* 2:23)? The world and all that is in it belongs to the Holy One, blessed be He. When He willed it, He gave it to you, and when he willed it, He took it away from you and gave it to us. And so it says, *The strength of His deeds He declared to His people*. G-d revealed to Yisrael the works of Creation in order *to give them the heritage of nations* (*Tehillim* 111:6).

I mentioned that the works of Creation remain a deep mystery even after the Torah describes them. This idea is found in *Bereishis Rabbah* and *Midrash Tanchuma* where it says: It is impossible to declare the power of the works of Creation to a human being. That's why the Torah simply says, *In the beginning G-d created*. Thus the words of the Sages confirm our explanation of the subject [that the story of Creation was written to substantiate Yisrael's claim to Eretz Yisrael, but the actual unfolding of the phases of Creation remains an unfathomable mystery].

THE PROCESS OF CREATION

1:1,2 **In the beginning G-d created the heaven and the earth. The earth was *tohu* and *bohu* and the darkness was on the face of the deep and the spirit of G-d was hovering over the water.**

. . . I will present the plain meaning of the verse, correctly and clearly. The Holy One, blessed be He, created the entire universe out of absolute nothingness. The only Hebrew expression for bringing forth something from nothing is the word *bara*, "He created." Everything that exists under the sun or above it did not come directly into being from nothingness. Rather, [G-d] brought forth from complete void and utter emptiness [only] a very delicate element. This element lacked substance but contained energy with the potential to take on form and convert into matter. This primordial matter is called *hiyuli* in Greek. After bringing *hiyuli* into being, G-d did not create anything, but He formed and made things with it. From this *hiyuli* He formed everything and clothed the forms and made them fit their function.

Realize that the heavens and all its components are made of one substance, and the earth and its components are made of one substance. The Holy One, blessed be He, created these two out of nothing;[14] only these two were created, everything else was fashioned from them. This primeval matter, which the Greeks called *hiyuli*, is called in Hebrew *tohu*. The word *tohu* is related to the word *betohei* in the Talmudic expression *betohei al harishonos*, "he regretted his former deeds." For if a person were to give a name [to this original matter], he is likely to regret his decision, have second thoughts, and call it by a different name, because [the prime substance] has not adopted a form to which the name could apply. The form which this original matter eventually adopts is called in Hebrew *bohu*, which is a combination of the two words *bo* and *hu*, "in it (*bo*) there is it (*hu*)" [in other words: the form is something that has substance to it.]

The plain meaning of the verses is as follows: *In the beginning G-d created the heaven,* meaning, He brought forth out of nothing the substance of heaven; *and the earth,* meaning, He brought forth out of nothing the substance of earth. *The earth* includes [not just earth but] all four elements [fire, air, water, and earth], as found in

---

14 *Ramban* explains: A tiny point smaller than a mustard seed developed into the heavens, and another point developed into the earth and all that is in it. These points are the *hiyuli* (primeval material) of heaven and earth (*Derashos HaRamban* 21).

the verse, *Heaven and earth were completed* (*Bereishis* 2:1) where earth includes the entire lower sphere [of existence]. We also find *Praise Hashem from the earth: sea giants and all watery depths* (*Tehillim* 148:7), and many other verses [indicating that earth refers to the whole world].

From this creation of formless primordial matter, which was like a tiny nonmaterial point, everything in heaven and earth was created. The Hebrew word for "the" is *es* which means the essence of the thing. The Sages said that the word *es* always comes to include something, for the Hebrew word *asah*—which has the same root as *es*—means came, as we find in the verse *"Morning came and also night"*. In our verse, *the heaven and the earth* too, the Rabbis expound that *es hashamayim*—the heaven—comes to include the sun, the moon, the stars, and the constellations; and the *es* of *haaretz*—the earth—comes to include the trees, the herbs, and *Gan Eden.* Thus, the two words *es* come to include all created things that have physical substance.

With one utterance G-d created the essence of heaven and earth and all their components. The verse then [continues "the earth was *tohu* and *bohu* and darkness was on the face of the deep and the spirit of G-d was hovering over the water"]. With the first step of creation the earth was *tohu*, it had only an intangible quality. When G-d gave it form, it became *bohu.*

This form included the four elements: fire, water, earth, and air, all of which are implicit in the word "earth". The element of fire is called "darkness" because essential fire is dark. Were fire to be essentially red, it would lend a red glare to the night. The element of water which was mixed with dust is called *the deep*. That's why the waters of the sea are called *the depths*, as in *The depths covered them* (*Shemos* 15:5); *The depths congealed* (*Shemos* 15:8); *The deep whirled around me* (*Yonah* 2:6). For this reason, the bottom of the sea is also called "the deep," as in *He roared at the Sea of Reeds and it became dry, and He led them through the depths as through a desert* (*Tehillim* 106:8), and, *Who led them through the depths as a horse through the desert* (*Yeshayah* 63:13). The element of air is called "spirit."

The four elements are one solid mass [without empty space between them]. The center of this mass is the earth; the sphere of water surrounds the earth; the sphere of air surrounds the water; and the sphere of fire surrounds the air. The Torah thus describes the earth's formation, as follows: the fire encircled the combination of water and dust, and the wind, blowing into the darkness hovered over the waters.

It seems to me that the ethereal point of *tohu* which took on form and became *bohu*, is what the Sages call *even shesiah*, "Foundation Stone," the nucleus around which the world was founded.

Thus the sense of the verses is: In the beginning G-d created the heavens out of nothing. The earth was also created out of nothing, first in a state of *tohu* and then becoming *bohu*. In this state it was composed of darkness [i.e., fire, as explained above], water, dust, and the wind, i.e., air, blowing on the waters. Thus was everything created. The word G-d [as the verse says *the spirit of G-d*] is attached to the element of "wind" and not to the other three elements because the element of wind—air, is the most ethereal and refined. It really should have been above the other three, but it hovered over the water—below the sphere of fire—by the command of the Holy One, blessed be He.

The creation of angels which are nonphysical beings, is not mentioned explicitly in the Torah, [although allusion to angels can be found].[15] The Sages expound that the angels were created on the second day, so no one could say they helped G-d create the world.

1:3 *Elohim* G-d—said, "There shall be Light," and light came into existence.

Elohim—The [Hebrew] word [for G-d] is *Elohim* which means "Master of all forces," since the root of *Elohim* is *ei-l*, meaning "force," and the word *Elohim* is a contraction of the words "force" and "they," alluding to all other forces. Thus *Elokim* means "the Force of all forces." We will explain this later on the basis of Kabbalah.[16]

---

15 *Zichron Yitzchak.*
16 In the commentary on verse 1:8, *G-d named the sky Heaven.*

G-d said "There shall be light"—The word "said" [in the context of Creation] means "want," as in, *Whatever your soul shall say I shall do for you* (1 *Shmuel* 20:4) meaning, "Whatever you want I shall do for you." Also, *Let her be a wife for your master's son, as G-d has said* (*Bereishis* 24:51), meaning, "as G-d wants it."

[The word "said" in the context of Creation may also mean] "think," as in, *Who says in her heart* (*Yeshayah* 47:8), and, *Then the captains of Yehudah will say in their hearts* (*Zechariah* 12:5). The Torah uses the word "said" [meaning think] to indicate that the creation of the world did not involve hard work. Our Rabbis too, interpreted "saying" [in this verse] as "thought", for they said: During the day [G-d] thought [of what to create], and created it in an instant at sunset. Thus the verse tells us that the creation was for a reason, not merely by G-d's desire.

1:26 Hashem said, "Let us make man with our image and our likeness. Let him dominate the fish of the sea, the birds of the sky, the livestock, land animals, and all the earth—and every animal that walks the earth."

Hashem said, "Let us make man"—G-d devoted a separate utterance to the creation of man [rather than including it in the verse, *The earth shall bring forth living creatures . . .* (1:24)] because of man's important status, for his is a different nature than the wild animals and cattle which G-d created in the previous utterance.

Let us make [in the plural rather than the singular] is explained as follows: I have already said [in verse 1:1] that G-d created [something from] nothing only on the first day. On the other days He formed and made things from the elements of [fire, wind, water, and earth]. On the fifth day, when G-d gave the water the power to bring forth living creatures, He said, *The waters shall teem* (1:20), and on the sixth day, when creating cattle, G-d said, *The earth shall bring forth* (1:24). Similarly, when G-d created man, He said, *Let us make,* as if to say: I and the abovementioned earth, will make man. How? The earth as it did with cattle and wild animals,

before it [at the end of the previous millennium] like we find that Avraham Avinu was born at the end of the second thousand years. There are many examples of major historic events of one millennium starting at the end of the previous millennium.

On the fourth day—the large light—[the sun], the small light—[the moon], and the stars were created. This "day" connotes the fourth thousand-year period. It started 72 years after the building of the first Beis Hamikdash[20] and ended 172 years after the destruction of the second Beis Hamikdash.[21] During that "day" the Jewish people enjoyed [spiritual] light, for the glory of G-d filled the House of G-d. G-d, the Light of Yisrael, was manifest in the fire on the Altar which crouched like a lion [in the first Bais Hamikdash] consuming the offerings. The small light [of the moon] represents the time G-d dimmed the light of Yisrael, for in the beginning of the era of the "small light" [of the moon] the Jews were banished from their land, just as the light of the moon disappears before the birth of the new moon. The "small light" eventually shone again during the period of the second Beis Hamikdash,[22] [in a diminished form] when the fire on the Altar took the shape of a dog.[23] Toward evening—at the end of the fourth millennium—the two lights faded away and the second Beis Hamikdash was destroyed.[24]

On the fifth day the water swarmed with living creatures, and fowl flew over the land. This signified the fifth thousand-year era which began 172 years after the destruction of the second Beis Hamikdash. During this millennium the nations will rule, and the Jews will be helpless *like the fish of the sea, like creeping things that have no ruler; [the nations] bring them all up with a fishhook, catch them in their net and gather them in their trawl (Chavakuk*

---

20 The first Beis Hamikdash was completed in the year 2928 of Creation.

21 The destruction of the second Beis Hamikdash was in the year 3828 of Creation (Rashi, *Avodah Zarah* 9a).

22 The small light symbolizes the second Beis Hamikdash and the reign of the Chashmonaim.

23 *Yoma* 21b. The second Beis Hamikdash was built by the Persians symbolized by a dog (*Rosh Hashanah* 4a).

24 In the year 3829 of Creation, 69 C.E.

1:14,15), and no one seeks G-d.

On the sixth day in the morning, G-d said, *Let the earth bring forth living creatures, each according to its kind* (1:24). This creation occurred before sunrise, as it says, *The sun rises and they are gathered in, and in their dens they crouch* (*Tehillim* 104:22). At sunrise, the beginning of the time of his dominion, man was created in the image of G-d, as it says in the next verse, *Man goes forth to his work and to his labor until evening.* This day represents the sixth thousand-year era. In the beginning of this period the wild beasts, i.e. the nations that do not know G-d will rule. After one-tenth of the day has passed, the time from daybreak until the first glimmer of the sun, the Redeemer will come, as it says [about the coming of Mashiach], *His throne shall be like the sun before Me* (*Tehillim* 89:37). This is the son of David who was formed in the image of G-d, as it says, *As I looked in the night vision, one like a man [i.e. Mashiach]; came with the clouds of heaven; he came up to the One of Ancient Days [i.e., G-d] and he was presented to Him. Dominion, glory and kingship were given to him* (*Daniel* 7:13,14). This will take place 118 years after the end of five thousand years,[25] the time of the Redemption G-d revealed to Daniel, in the verse, *From the time the daily offering was removed [at the destruction of the second Beis Hamikdash] and the mute abomination was put in place, one thousand two hundred and ninety years* (*Daniel* 12:11).

Since the fish and fowl were created on the fifth day, while the beasts of the earth were created on the sixth day, it seems that in the beginning of the sixth millennium a new world power will arise—*fearful, dreadful, and very powerful* (*Daniel* 7:7) which will be closer to the truth than the nations before it.[26]

The seventh day—Shabbos—alludes to the World to Come, a day of complete Shabbos and rest for eternal life. May G-d watch over us all the days and grant our share with His servants, the perfect ones.

---

[25] i.e., the year 5118 from Creation, or 1358 C.E. It should be noted that the Ramban lived from 1195 to 1270 C.E.

[26] Referring to the Arab nations who believe in G-d and do not worship idols.

THE EXALTEDNESS OF THE SOUL

2:7 Hashem, God, formed man from dust of the ground and breathed into his nostrils the soul of life; and man became a living being.

He breathed into his nostrils the soul of life—This phrase characterizes the loftiness of the soul, its foundation and mystery. The verse associates the soul with G-d's name as it says *Hashem, God formed man*, by breathing into man's nostrils the soul of life. Man's soul did not come to him from the four elements, as opposed to the life force of animals [which does come from the four elements], nor did it evolve from angels. It is the spirit of G-d alone, from whose mouth come knowledge and understanding. One who breathes into someone else's nostrils gives him something of his own soul, as it says, *It is the soul of the Al-mighty that gives them understanding* (*Iyov* 32:8).

Great thinkers differ regarding the nature of the soul. Some say that man has three souls: The first is the soul or the power of growth which makes plants grow. The second is the soul of motion which the Torah calls "living being" when referring to fish, beasts, and creeping things. The third is the rational soul, [by which man can think and speak].

Others believe that man's rational soul, given to him from the Almighty, is one soul comprising three forces. The plain meaning of the verse suggests this, as it says, *G-d formed man out of dust of the ground*, and man lay there like a lifeless chunk of stone, until the Holy One, blessed be He, breathed into his nostrils the soul of life. Then, *man became a living being,* meaning, he was he able to move, as we find this term regarding animals and fish about which G-d said, *Let the waters teem with teeming living creatures* (1:20), and *Let the earth bring forth living creatures* (1:24), meaning, creatures that can move. Accordingly, we infer that man was transformed from a potsherd of earth into a living being only through the soul he was given.[27]

---

[27] There are other examples where the *lamed* transforms something into its opposite, such as, *The water will turn into blood* (ledam) (*Shemos* 4:9); *it turned into a snake* (lenachash), (*Shemos* 4:3); *He turned the sea to damp land* (lecharavah) (*Shemos* 14:21).

However Onkelos translates: *man became a living being* as "*it became a speaking soul in man*" [implying that his life force preceded this soul, and this soul only gave him the power to speak.] This indicates that he is of the opinion that man has various souls, and the rational soul which G-d breathed into his nostrils was his speaking soul.

It seems to me that [the idea of multiple souls] is also the opinion of our Rabbis. For we read in the Gemara: Rava created a man[28] and sent him to Rav Zeira, who spoke to the man, but he did not answer. Said Rav Zeira, "I see that you were created by one of our colleagues. Go back to your dust!"[29]

This [that man has multiple souls] is also seen in Vayikra Rabbah: Rabbi Avin said: When a man sleeps, the body—the vegetative soul, tells the *neshamah*—the soul of motion, which tells the *nefesh*—the rational soul, which tells the angel.

Accordingly the verse, *Hashem God formed man* refers to the formation of the body, and the formation of the soul of motion, conveying the idea that G-d made man capable of movement, since "formation" implies life and perception, making him a man and not a mass of dust, as it says, [concerning other living creatures] *Hashem, God had formed out of the ground every beast of the field and every bird of the sky, and brought them to the man* (2:19). After giving man the power of perception, G-d breathed into his nostrils a living soul—the rational soul—in addition to the soul of motion which he already had. Thereby *man became a living being* capable of understanding, speaking, and acting, for all the other souls and their powers are under the control of the rational soul.[30] Or we

---

[28] Using the Sefer Yetzirah, a Kabbalistic work attributed to Avraham Avinu.

[29] This Gemara supports the view that the soul consists of three different parts. For Rava was able to give the man the soul of motion, but he was unable to give him the power of speech which is seated in the G-d given rational soul (*R. Bachya* on verse 12:2).

[30] The letter lamed in the word *lenefesh* denotes ownership, as in the following verses: *My lord the king; "lecha ani" I am yours, and all I own [is yours] (1 Melachim 20:4); "lakoneh oso" to the one who purchased it (Vayikra 25:30).* Accordingly we interpret the verse "man became owned or acquired by the living soul."

may interpret the verse to mean that man became another person, completely transformed into a living soul, for now, whatever he did was directed toward this soul.

The Tree of Knowledge

2:9 Hashem, G-d, made grow out of the ground every tree that is pleasant to look at and good to eat, including the Tree of Life in the middle of the garden, and the Tree of Knowledge of good and evil.

the Tree of Life—The fruit of this tree gave long life to one who ate from it.

the Tree of Knowledge of good and evil—The commentators say that those eating its fruit desired sexual intercourse, therefore Adam and Chavah covered their nakedness after eating its fruit. They quote another instance [where "good and evil" refers to desire], when Barzilai HaGiladi said: [*I have aged,*] *can I distinguish good from evil?* (2 Shmuel 19:36), meaning his sexual desire left him. I consider this interpretation [that "good and evil" refers to desire] incorrect, because the serpent said to Chavah, [if you eat from the tree,] *You will be like G-d, knowing good and evil* (3:5) meaning: "You will become like angels knowing good and evil." [Surely angels do not have sexual desires,] therefore, "good and evil" cannot refer to this desire. Do not debate this, saying the serpent lied [when it said: You will be like G-d,] for the Torah itself says, *G-d said "Man has now become like one of us in knowing good and evil"* (3:22). Furthermore the Rabbis comment: Three spoke the truth and perished from the world: the serpent, the spies,[31] and Doeg HaEdomi.[32]

---

[31] *Bamidbar* ch. 13 and 14.
[32] 1 *Shmuel* 22:9-10.

I think, that before eating from the Tree of Knowledge, doing the right thing came naturally to man, just as the sun and the stars perform their assigned tasks without deviating, [following their orbits] uninfluenced by love or hate. The fruit of the tree stimulated will and desire, causing those who ate from it to choose either good or evil. Therefore it is called the tree of Knowledge of good and evil, for Knowledge is an expression of "will." For example, in *Tanach*, we find, *G-d, what is a man that you should know him* (*Tehillim* 143:3) which means "that You should desire and want him;" *I know you by name* (*Shemos* 33:12) which means "I have chosen you of all people." Similarly, Barzilai's statement, *"can I know between good and evil"* means that he lost the power of will, no longer choosing or avoiding something, he ate without tasting and heard singing without enjoyment.

[Before eating the forbidden fruit] marital relations between Adam and his wife was not a matter of desire; rather, they united and procreated when they wanted offspring. Therefore, all their limbs were in their eyes, like their face and hands, and they were unashamed of them. But after eating from the Tree of Knowledge, Adam was given the power of choice; now he could willingly do evil or good to himself or to others. Though choice is a Divine attribute, it can be bad for man, for through choice, he has temptation and desire. It is possible that *Koheles* had this in mind when he said, *G-d made man upright, but they sought many designs* (*Koheles* 7:29). Man is "upright" when he keeps to the one right path, but when he "seeks many designs," his search for actions can change according to his free choice.

G-d commanded Adam to avoid eating the fruit of the Tree, without informing him that it gave one freedom of choice. He merely told him, *But of the fruit of the tree that is in the middle of the garden, [the tree known by its central location], you may not eat from it.* And this was what the woman repeated to the serpent. The verse, *But of the Tree of Knowledge of good and evil, you must not eat from it*, which describes the tree's ability to grant one choice, was only related to us, not told to Adam.

MAN IS DESTINED TO DIE

2:17 But from the Tree of Knowledge of good and evil, do not eat, for on the day you eat from it, you will definitely die.

On the day you eat from it, you will definitely die—[The verse does not mean that one who eats from it will die immediately, rather] when one eats from it, he will be liable to death. In the same vein [Shlomoh said to Shim'i,] *On the day that you leave [Yerushalayim] to go here or there, you should know well that you will surely die* (1 *Melachim* 2:42). Shlomoh did not mean that Shim'i would die as soon as he left Yerushalayim. Nor did he mean to tell [Shim'i] he would die [in the future,] for everyone knows that man will die. He meant to tell [Shim'i] that as soon as he left Yerushalayim, he was liable to the death penalty, and the king would execute him when he so pleased. This is also the meaning of the following verses, *[The Kehosites] will then not come and see the sacred furnishings being packed, and they will not die (Bamidbar 4:20),* and . . . *which is a sin that can cause them to die (Vayikra 22:9).* [Those who transgress will not die immediately], rather they will die because of the sin they committed.

According to the physicians,[33] man was destined to die from the beginning of his formation, because he is made up of the four elements [and any combination of elements breaks down into its original parts. Therefore the verse can't mean only if you eat from it, will you eventually die]. Rather, G-d decreed that if man sinned, he would die because of his sin. Whenever the Torah decrees that one is liable to death at the hands of Heaven, such as a non-kohen eating *terumah,*[34] a kohen who drank wine or did not wear the [required number of] priestly garments when performing the service

---

[33] The Greek physician Galen, one of the most distinguished physicians of antiquity (129-199 c.e.)

[34] *Terumah* is a portion of the crops which must be separated and given to the kohanim (*Bamidbar* 18:12).

in the *Beis Hamikdash,* and other such cases, it must be understood that as punishment, they will die earlier than anticipated. When stating Adam's punishment G-d added, *Finally you will return to the ground, for it was from [the ground] that you were taken. You are dust, and to dust you shall return* (3:19), meaning that Adam from his creation by nature would die. [Additionally] even before he sinned, Adam ate fruit and seeds of the earth (1:29), [proving that] the four elements—the building blocks of his body—were deteriorating steadily, and he had to eat to replace the dwindling substances. [This is the view of the physicians.]

However our Rabbis say, had Adam not sinned, he would never have died, because his higher soul would have given him everlasting life. The spirit of G-d within him since his creation, would have clung to him, causing him to live forever.

The theory that all matter is composed of the four elements which disintegrate over time, was postulated by men of little faith who believe that creation came about as a matter of necessity[35] [not as a result of G-d's design, choice, and desire]. But men of faith believe that the world [had a beginning,] was created by the will of G-d, and will exist as long as G-d wants. This is the obvious truth. Thus, the passage, *On the day you eat from it, you will definitely die* means if you eat from it, you will be liable to death; by My will you will not live forever. [We must say that Adam did not eat in order to exist, for he lived by the will of G-d,] rather he ate originally for enjoyment. Possibly the fruits of Gan Eden were absorbed in Adam's limbs like the manna which fell in the desert and sustained those that ate it, [not naturally but through the spiritual quality of the fruit]. But when [he sinned and was driven out of Gan Eden,] G-d decreed that he eat the grass of the field and bread by the sweat of his brow, causing his body to deteriorate. [According to this interpretation, only because of his sin does the Torah say] *you are dust and to dust you shall return.*

---

35   This is the opinion of Aristotle (*Moreh Nevuchim* 2:19).

A COMPANION FOR ADAM

2:18 Hashem said, "It is not good for man to be alone. I will make a helper to face him."

It is not good for man to be alone—It seems unlikely that man was created to be alone in the world incapable of begetting children, since all living things of all species were created male and female to have offspring. Herbs and trees, were also created bearing their own kinds of seeds. It is possible to explain man's creation according to the view of R. Yirmeyah b. Eliezer who said: G-d created Adam originally with two profiles. A reproductive force or perhaps a seed, could pass from his male part to his female part as debated by the scientists on the nature of pregnancy.[36] The second profile [of man] helped the first profile to beget offspring. G-d saw that it would be good for the "helper" to face the man, so he could see [it] and separate or connect with it as he wished. Thus, the verse says, *I will make a helper to face him* [meaning: I will make the helper who is now attached in back of him, face him, unattached.]

[Why was man as a single two part creation called "not good"?] Man in his single two part state, could not be described with the phrase "it was good", for he did not continue to exist in this form. The phrase "it was good" during the work of Creation means it achieved its final form, as I have explained on the verse, *And G-d saw that it was good* (1:10).

2:24 A man shall therefore leave his father and his mother and cling to his wife, and they shall become one flesh.

And cling to his wife, and they shall become one flesh— According to Rashi, "one flesh" refers to the child wherein their flesh becomes united. But this does not stand to reason, because

---

[36] The Ramban discusses this in the beginning of *parashas Tazria*.

even cattle and beasts [which do not cling to their mates] become united in their offspring.

In think the correct interpretation is as follows: Male animals do not bond with females. Rather, the animals mate and go different ways. [By contrast,] Adam's wife was "bone from his bone and flesh from his flesh," therefore he would cling to her, loving her as his own flesh, and wanting to be with her always. Adam's nature, is ingrained in his offspring, therefore males leave their fathers and mothers, clinging to their wives, and considering them their own flesh. In fact, by leaving his father and mother man shows that his wife is closer to him than his parents are.

We find in the Torah that close relatives are called "near of flesh." For example, *After all, he is our brother, our own flesh* (*Bereishis* 37:27), and *No person shall approach his near of flesh* meaning a close relative (*Vayikra* 18:6).

GAN EDEN ON EARTH AND IN HEAVEN

3:22 G-d said, "Man has now become like one of us in knowing good and evil. Now he must be prevented from putting forth his hand and also taking from the Tree of Life. He [can] eat it and live forever!"

Know and believe that Gan Eden is on earth, the Tree of Life and the Tree of Knowledge are in it, and a river *which divides into four major rivers* (2:10) which can be seen by us, flows from it. The Euphrates River is within the borders of our land, and, the river Pishon is the Nile in Egypt according to the early commentators.[37]

These creations on earth have counterparts in heaven with the same names, which are the foundation and root of their counterparts on earth. The Rabbis comment on the verse, *The King has brought me into His chambers* (*Shir Hashirim* 1:4)—In time to come, the Holy One, blessed be He, will show Yisrael the treasures

---

[37] Rashi, R. Saadiah Gaon and the *Zohar* 1:125.

on high, stored in the chambers of heaven. According to another interpretation, *The King has brought me into His chambers* refers to the chambers of Gan Eden. In light of this the Sages said: Spiritual things in the higher world correspond to material things in the Gan Eden of this world.

The four rivers match the four camps of the *Shechinah* on high; it is from there that the kingdoms of earth draw strength, as it says, *With the hosts of heaven in heaven, and with the kings of earth on earth* (*Yeshayah* 24:21). And so the rabbis said: The *four major rivers* are the four kingdoms. *The name of the first is Pishon* this is Babylon . . . The things called the Tree of Life and the Tree of Knowledge in heaven are a high and exalted secret.

What Caused Man's Lifespan to Shrink?

5:4   **Adam lived 800 years after he had Shes, and he had sons and daughters.**

Because the first men lived so long, the Torah lists their ages before they fathered children, how long they lived afterward, and the total number of years they lived. This continued until the generation after the flood.

The reason they lived so long is because Adam, the handiwork of the Holy One, blessed be He, was flawless in beauty, strength, and height. Even after he was punished with mortality, it was in his nature to live a long time. But once the flood covered the earth, the air degenerated, causing man's lifespan gradually to shrink. Until the flood, people's lifespans were similar to Adam's, with some living even longer.

Shem, born before the flood, lived 600 years, [which was less than the generations before him but more than the generations after him], for he was born during the period when people were still stronger. But [after the flood] the polluted air affected him. The life span of his children born after the flood was 400 years.

This life span remained the norm until the generation of the Dispersion,[38] when the change in climate caused by the Dispersion shortened their lives even more. For Peleg, in whose days the world was divided, lived only 200 years, half as long as the preceding generations. In the days of Avraham, Yitzchak, and Yaakov, it seems that people lived seventy to eighty years, as Moshe Rabbeinu mentions in his prayer Tefillah LeMoshe.[39] The Patriarchs who were the righteous men of their generations, [lived longer, because] the fear of Hashem increased their days. Thus Pharaoh wondered about Yaakov's old age, and Yaakov countered with the even greater wonder that his forefathers lived longer, as he said, *I did not live as long as my fathers did during their pilgrimage through life* (47:9).

The Rambam, in *Moreh Nevuchim* (2:27) writes that only the individuals mentioned in the Torah lived long, either due to their life-style and diet, or because of a miracle. The rest of the generation lived a normal age. I do not agree. Why perform a miracle for those that were neither prophets nor righteous, and unworthy of miracles; especially for generation after generation. Furthermore, how could life-style and diet prolong their lives many times more than the rest of their generation? In addition, why wouldn't other people follow this regimen, in order to reach the same venerable age. Finally, why wasn't this wholesome way of life passed on to even one of the descendants of Noach after the flood [so he could live as long as his ancestors]? True, wisdom diminishes steadily from generation to generation, but some wisdom [regarding healthful practices] should have remained.

---

[38] The generation that built the Tower of Babel (*Bereishis* 11:1-8).
[39] *Tehillim* 90:10.

נח
NOACH

———•◦•———

THE ENORMOUS SHIPLOAD OF THE ARK

6:19 From all that lives, of all flesh, bring two of each kind into the ark to keep them alive with you. They shall be male and female.

There are countless species of beasts, some as large as elephants, and there are myriads of creeping things and fowl, as our Rabbis say: "There are one hundred and twenty kinds of unclean birds in the east, all of them belonging to the species of *ayah* (vulture) [which is only one of the species of unclean fowl]; the number of clean fowl is endless." Noach had to bring [two of] every kind into the ark, so they could breed [and be preserved]. Add to that the food needed for them to last an entire year, and you will find that even ten arks of this size[40] could not contain it all. Surely, it was only through a miracle that such a small space held so large a volume.

If the ark could not contain the bulk naturally, why didn't Noach make the ark even smaller and rely on this miracle? G-d wanted Noach to make such a large ark so that the people of his generation would see it, wonder about it, discuss it, and talk about the forthcoming flood and the gathering of animals into it, and perhaps repent.

---

[40] The ark was 300 cubits long, 50 cubits wide and 30 cubits high.

A large ark also scales down the miracle, and all miracles in the Torah or Prophets, are performed only after man has done his utmost. Don't be won over [by the commentary of Ibn Ezra] who describes the 300 cubits [of the length of the ark] as cubits relative to the size of the exceptionally tall Noach, for were this to be so, his contemporaries and the beasts and fowl would also be oversized [and still be unable to fit into the ark]. Besides [Ibn Ezra's commentary is not acceptable] because all cubits mentioned in the Torah are standard cubits.

TWO CAME OF THEIR OWN ACCORD

6:20 From each separate species of bird, from each separate species of livestock, and from each thing that creeps on the ground, two of each shall come to you to keep alive.

Two of each shall come to you to keep alive—G-d told Noach that two of every species would come of their own accord to be brought into the ark; he would not have to hunt for them in the mountains and faraway places. In verse [7:9], the Torah tells us that these two came male and female, which was true of all species, without exception. Next, G-d told Noach to take seven and seven[41] of every clean animal. Here the Torah does not say they "shall come" which would indicate that they came on their own, rather Noach had to take them. For only those animals saved from the flood [for their own good] to keep their seed alive, came of their own accord, but the other pairs which were brought in order for Noach to bring sacrifices, G-d did not decree that they come voluntarily to be slaughtered.[42] Noach took them, since he would bring a sacrifice from them after the flood.

---

[41] Six pairs in addition to the one pair that came on their own accord to preserve the species.

[42] The Ramban (7:8) explains because this was a mitzvah, Hashem wanted Noach to be busy with the mitzvah. R. Bachya explains that G-d took pity on the animals and did not compel them to come voluntarily to be sacrificed.

G-D REMEMBERED NOACH

8:1 G-d remembered Noach and all the beasts and all the animals that were with him in the ark, and G-d made a wind blow on the earth, and the waters subsided.

G-d remembered Noach and all the beast and all the animals— Because Noach was a faultlessly righteous man, G-d remembered and made a pact with him to save him (6:18). The word "Noach" includes his children who were with him in the ark. The Torah does not mention them by name, because they were only saved in his merit. Only man has merit or guilt therefore we cannot say G-d remembered the beasts and animals because of any merit on their part. G-d remembered them in the sense that *He remembered His holy promise* (*Tehillim* 105:42) which He made when He created the world, wanting the world to continue to exist with all the species created in it. Therefore, G-d saw fit to bring them out of the ark. The Torah does not mention that G-d remembered the fowl and the creeping things, for they are included in the remembrance of the beasts and animals.

WHERE DID THE DOVE FIND THE OLIVE LEAF?

8:11 The dove returned to him toward evening, and there was a freshly plucked olive leaf in its beak. Noach then knew that the water had subsided from the earth.

and there was a freshly-plucked olive leaf in its beak—The plain meaning of this passage indicates that the trees were not uprooted or destroyed in the flood. Since the whole world was flooded with water [simultaneously], there were no raging streams to rip them out.

But in *Bereishis Rabbah* (33:9) the Rabbis ask: From where did the dove bring the olive leaf? R. Levi said: She brought it from the Mount of Olives, because Eretz Yisrael was not swamped by the

Waters of the flood. And so said G-d to Yechezkel, *Son of man, say to her (Yerushalayim) You are a land that has not been cleansed, that has not been rained upon on the day of fury (Yechezkel 22:24)*. R. Bibi said: The gates of Gan Eden were opened for the dove, and she brought the leaf from there. Thus according to the Rabbis, the trees were uprooted and destroyed in those places where the flood was, and surely the leaves withered. In the same vein, the Rabbis said: Even the lower millstones dissolved in the flood. As proof they cite the verse, *Stones are worn away by water (Iyov 14:19)*.

R. Levi [who said the dove brought the leaf from the Mount of Olives] opines that the flood rains did not come down on Eretz Yisrael, as it says, [*Yerushalayim*] *has not been rained upon*, nor did the wellsprings of the great deep burst forth on it. But R. Levi must admit that the waters which inundated the other countries covering the highest mountains, as related in verse 7:19, [must have covered Eretz Yisroel for] there was no protective dam around Eretz Yisrael to prevent the waters from coming in. Indeed, *Pirkei D'Rabbi Eliezer* states that: The rains of the Flood did not fall on Eretz Yisrael, but the water from the other countries streamed into it. Thus R. Levi believes that since the heavy rains did not come down on Eretz Yisrael, and the floodgate of heaven did not open on it, the trees survived,[43] while the trees in the rest of the world were uprooted and destroyed by the flood and torrential rains.

I am puzzled by [R. Bibi's statement that the leaf was] from Gan Eden. Since the waters of the flood never entered Gan Eden how could Noach infer from this that the water had subsided from the earth. Perhaps its gates were closed during the flood, and only when the waters subsided were they opened.

[Since the trees in the world were uprooted and destroyed during the flood,] the Rabbis in *Bereishis Rabbah*, commenting on the verse, *[Noach] planted a vineyard (9:20)* asked: Where did he find a vine? R. Abba b. Kahana said: Noach brought the vine, shoots of fig trees, and stumps of olive trees into the ark.

---

43   Because the seething waters flowing in, had a chance to cool off.

dants of Cham . . . by their lands and nations (10:19,20). The same
is true of the descendants of Shem.[46]

WHY THE TORAH RECORDS THE HISTORY
OF THE NATIONS

The Torah details the lineage [of Noach sons] to inform us how
Avraham descends from Shem. Cham's descendants are mentioned to let the world know that Avraham was granted possession
of their lands because of the sins of their fathers. The account of
Yefes and the dispersion (11:1-9) lets us know how the languages
diverged and the nations spread to the ends of the earth within a
short period of time after Adam HaRishon.[47]

Additionally, the story of the children of Noach, makes us aware
of G-d's kindness; He kept the covenant He made with Noach not
to destroy his offspring, [for by listing the nations, we see they are
indeed in existence].

THE TIMELINE

The Rambam, in *Moreh Nevuchim* (3:50) says that the Torah lists
the families descended from Noach including their names and
territories to prove that the universe was created out of nothing.
This is also confirmed by our father Avraham who commanded his
children and his household after him, vouching that Noach and his
sons saw the flood and were in the ark. Avraham [although he did

---

[46] As can be seen from verse 30, *Their settlements extended form Meshah toward
Sefer*, all located on the Arabian peninsula.
[47] Ordinarily, a person's descendants speak his language and settle nearby. The fact
that people speak different languages and are scattered all over the globe may mislead people into thinking that mankind descended from more than one ancestor.
For this reason the Torah relates that until the dispersion everyone spoke the same
language and lived in the same area.

not see the flood] heard the direct testimony of witnesses who were there. He was also a fourth hand witness to Creation, [for Avraham saw] Noach who saw his father Lemech who saw Adam.[48] Yitzchak and Yaakov [themselves] saw Shem,[49] who was in the ark during the flood. Yaakov told this to his children who went down to Egypt. He also told it to Pharaoh and the people of his generation.

In every generation fathers teach their descendants about their genealogy, about things that happened four or five generations ago, and about the things their ancestors did.

AVRAHAM'S PLACE OF BIRTH

11:28 Haran died during the lifetime of his father Terach, in the land of his birth, Ur Kasdim.

During the lifetime of his father Terach, in the land of his birth—Rashi, quoting the Midrash, explains that Terach caused Haran's death. Terach complained to Nimrod that Avraham had smashed his idols, and Nimrod threw Avraham into a fiery furnace. Meanwhile, Haran [his brother] wavered, saying to himself, "If Avram wins I will be on his side, and if Nimrod wins, I will be on his side." When Avram was saved, they asked Haran, "Whose side are you on?" Replied Haran, "I'm on Avram's side." They threw him into the furnace, and he died in the fire.[50] Therefore it is called *Ur Kasdim*—the fire of Kasdim—[for the Hebrew word Ur means fire.]

---

[48] Avraham lived from 1948-2123 from Creation. Noach lived from 1056-2006. The flood was in 1656. Thus Avraham knew Noach, since he was 58 years old when Noach died. Noach's father Lemech was born in 874, and Adam died in 930, thus Lemech knew Adam for the first 56 years of his life. The dispersion was in 1996 (Artscroll *Tanach,* Timeline 1).

[49] Shem lived from 1558-2158 from Creation. Yitzchak lived from 2048-2228, and Yaakov 2108-2255. Thus both Yitzchak and Yaakov saw Shem who was in the ark.

[50] Since Haran defied Nimrod not because of his belief, but because he expected a miracle, he was unworthy of one.

However Menachem[51] defines *ur* as "valley," . . . for every hole or deep gorge is called *ur*. But the tradition we received from our Rabbis [that *Ur Kasdim* means the fiery furnace of Kasdim] is the truth, as I will explain.

[Although the verse "in the land of his birth in Ur Kasdim" seems to indicate that Avraham was born in Ur Kasdim, this cannot be so, for] our father Avraham was not born in Kasdim (Chaldea). Chaldea and the land of Shinar were inhabited by the sons of Cham while Avram was a descendant of Shem.[52] The verse, *He brought the news to Avram the Ivri* (the Hebrew) (14:13), not Avram the Kasdi (Chaldean) [is another proof that he was not born in Kasdim]. Furthermore, it says, *Your forefathers—Terach, the father of Avraham and the father of Nachor—[Avraham's brother]—always dwelled on the other side of the [Euphrates] River* (*Yehoshua* 24:2). The word *always* teaches us that Terach lived there for ages. Additionally, it says, *But I took your forefather Avraham from the other side of the River* (24:3), [which proves he was not born in Kasdim].

Moreover Terach left Ur Kasdim with Avram, Lot, and Sarai [but not Nachor]. Were Terach's origins in Ur Kasdim, we must say that Nachor stayed there. Yet we find (29:4,5) that Nachor lived in Charan!

In fact, Terach, Avraham, and Nachor were born in Aram, on the other side of the River [Euphrates in Mesopotamia]. This was their hereditary property since time immemorial, as we learn from the verse concerning the descendants of Shem, *Their dwelling place extended from Mesha going toward Sefar, the mountain of the east* (10:30). *The mountain of the east* is a general term for the entire region encompassing all their countries, as it says, *by their lands and nations* (10:31). Furthermore it says, *Balak, king of Moav, has brought me from Aram, from the mountains of the east* (*Bamidbar* 23:7). Since Aram is in the land of "the mountain of the east,"

---

[51]   Menachem b. Saruk, a great grammarian from the 10th century.
[52]   See 10:10-12, and *the land of his birth, Ur Kasdim* refers to the land of Haran's birth *(Tur)*.

Avraham and his ancestors must have lived in the land of Aram.

The Talmud (Bava Basra 91a) says that Avraham was confined in Kutah. This city is not in Kasdim (Chaldea), for it says, *The King of Ashur (Assyria) brought [people] from Babylonia and Kutah . . . and he settled them in the cities of Shomron* (2 *Melachim* 17:24). And it says further, *The people of Babylonia made Sukkos-Benos; the people of Kutah made Nergal* (17:30). Kutah appears to be a city on the other side of the River in the land of Aram Naharaim (Mesopotamia), Charan is a city in Aram Naharaim [and we may assume that Kutah is there too], for it says, [*Eliezer, Avraham's servant*] *set off and went to Aram Naharaim, to the city of Nachor* (*Bereishis* 24:10), which is Charan.

Furthermore, we heard from many students who used to live in that country, that Kutah is a large city between Charan and Ashur, far from the country of Babylonia. The distance between Kutah and Charan is approximately a six-day journey. Nevertheless, it is included in the term "on the other side of the river," because it lies between the two rivers, i.e., between the Euphrates (*Peros*), which is the border of Eretz Yisrael, and the Tigris (*Chidekel*) which flows toward the east of Ashur (Assyria).

[To summarize:] Terach fathered his older sons, Avraham and Nachor in the region "on the other side of the river," in the land of his ancestors. He went with his son Avram to the land of Kasdim (Chaldea). There his younger son Haran was born. His son Nachor remained "on the other side of the river" in the city of Charan. It is possible that he was born there, or that he settled there, coming from Kutah. Therefore, the passage, *in the land of his birth, Ur Kasdim*, refers to Haran, since [of Terach's three sons] only Haran was born there.

AVRAHAM'S FAITH MENTIONED IN NON-JEWISH BOOKS

These events in the life of Avraham, which we know by tradition from our Rabbis, are found in ancient non-Jewish chronicles.

The Rambam, in *Moreh Nevuchim* writes (3:29) that "The Egyptian Agriculture"[53] relates that Avraham was born in Kutah, opposed the idolatrous views of the masses who worshipped the sun, and was put in prison. Because he debated with the authorities, the king, afraid Avram would undermine his authority and cause people to abandon their religion, banished him to the far-away land of Canaan after seizing all his wealth.

Certainly, a miracle happened to Avraham in the land of Kasdim. According to the non-Jewish book, it was a hidden miracle because G-d had the king decide to release Avrohom from prison, sending him on his way rather than killing him. According to our Rabbis it was an overt miracle, because the king threw him into the fiery furnace and he was saved.

Rabbi Avraham ibn Ezra questions why the text does not mention this miracle. Later on[54] I will explain why the Torah does not relate this and similar miracles.

WHY THE TORAH DOES NOT MENTION AVRAHAM'S MIRACLE

The non-Jews do not mention the miracle [of Avraham emerging from the furnace unscathed] because they disagreed with Avraham's outlook, believing that Avraham's miracle was made through sorcery, like the Egyptians first thought about Moshe's miracles.

The Torah does not mention this miracle because it would have had to mention also the opposing view, as it mentioned the words of the Egyptian sorcerers, and Avraham's belief was not substantiated as Moshe's words were proved to be true.

[After Avraham was saved from the furnace of Kasdim,] G-d said to him, *I am Hashem who brought you out of Ur Kasdim to give you*

---

[53] In *Moreh Nevuchim* the Rambam calls the book "The Nabatean Agriculture."
[54] (46:15)

this land as a possession (15:7). G-d did not say "I took you out from Ur Kasdim" [indicating a natural event] rather He said "I brought you out", implying that G-d brought him out like a prisoner from confinement miraculously, as in the verse, *Who brought you out of Egypt, from the place of slavery* (*Shemos* 20:2). From the passage, *to give you this land as a possession*, we learn it was G-d's will to make Avraham into a great nation, giving him this land, from the time He brought him out of Ur Kasdim.

Immediately after Avraham was saved, he and his father Terach, afraid of the king, wanted to remove to Canaan, far from the land of Kasdim. Because Charan was close to Kasdim, both people sharing the same nationality and language, they did not want to go to Avraham's birthplace Charan.[55] Rather, they preferred a nation whose language the king and his people did not understand [making it difficult to send agents to capture and bring them back to Kasdim].

The verse, *They departed with them from Ur Kasdim to go to the land of Canaan; they arrived at Charan, and settled there* (11:31), means that en route to Canaan they stopped in Charan where their families and ancestors had always lived, settling among them for a long time. There, Avraham was commanded to go to the land of Canaan which he had indeed intended. He left his father who died in Charan, his homeland, and went with his wife and nephew Lot to the land of Canaan. And so it says, *I took your forefather Avraham from on the other side of the River and led him throughout all the land of Canaan* (*Yehoshua* 24:3). It was "on the other side of the River" where Avraham received this command, [not in Ur Kasdim], and from there G-d led him throughout the land of Canaan.

To summarize: The Rabbis [quoted by Rashi] understand *Ur Kasdim* according to its plain meaning "Fire of Kasdim," as in, *I have warmed myself, I see the* [ur] *flame* (*Yeshayah* 44:16).

---

55 They were afraid that the king would reconsider and have them arrested in Charan.

Although Terach did not emerge from the fiery furnace he is included in the verse that says, *They departed with them from Ur Kasdim* (11:31) because Avraham the main character emerged from the furnace.

Alternatively, the place itself was named *Ur Kasdim* because of the miracle that happened there, [and it can therefore properly be said, that Terach too, left Ur Kasdim]. [We often find places named after events that happened there,] such as Tav'erah, Massah, Kivros Hataavah (*Devarim* 9:22) and other verses. When Avraham emerged from the fiery furnace they all fled from there.

לך לך

LECH LECHA

A SIGN FOR THE CHILDREN

12:6 Avram traveled through the land as far as the site of Shechem, coming to the Plain of Moreh. The Canaanites were then in the land.

Avram traveled through the land as far as the site of Shechem—A fundamental principle to understand portions of the Torah relating events of Avraham, Yitzchok and Yaakov, is stated by our Rabbis: "Whatever happened to the Fathers is a sign for the children." Therefore the verses expand upon the journeys of the Patriarchs, the digging of the wells, and other events which at first glance seem unnecessary. By reflecting about events that happened to any of the three Patriarchs, we can understand things that were decreed for their future children.

THE SIGNIFICANCE OF SYMBOLIC ACTS

[The Ramban explains why G-d had the Patriarchs personally experience events that would befall their children rather than telling them about it in a prophetic vision.]

A heavenly decree that is actualized symbolicly will be fulfilled in all its aspects. For this reason, the prophets performed symbolic acts about the message they were prophesying. For example, Yirmeyah commanded Seraiah, *And then, when you finish reading this book, tie a stone into it and throw it into the midst of the Euphrates, and say: "Thus shall Babylon sink and not rise"* (*Yirmeyah* 51:63). So too, Elisha placed his hand on the hands of King Yehoash [who was holding the bow] telling him: *"Shoot!" and he shot. [Elisha] then said, "It is an arrow of victory for Hashem, and an arrow of victory over Aram." Then he said, "Now pick up the arrows," and he picked them up. He said to the king of Yisrael, "Strike [the arrows] to the ground!" and he struck three times and stopped. The man of G-d became angry with him and said, "Had you only struck five or six times! Then you would have annihilated Aram; as it is, you shall defeat Aram only three times"* (2 *Melachim* 13:16-19).

Therefore the Holy One, blessed be He, made Avraham take possession of the Land experiencing events that foreshadowed things destined to happen in the future to his children. This is the principle. With G-d's help I will explain in detail the subject matter of the verses also.

AN OVERVIEW

A vram traveled through the land as far as the area of Shechem—Rashi says: Avraham entered [the city of Shechem] to pray for Yaakov's sons who would come distressed from the field [and do battle against Shechem]. This is correct. I add, that Avraham took possession of [Shechem] before G-d told him He would give him the land. This foreshadowed the conquering and destruction of Shechem by his sons[56] even before the land was given to them, and before the sins of its inhabitants had reached full measure to warrant their expulsion. Thus the verse says, *The Canaanites were then in the land* [meaning: Even though the

---

[56] Avenging the rape of their sister Dinah, Shimon and Levi wiped out Shechem (34:25,26).

Canaanites were then in the land, Avraham took possession of Shechem, thereby making it possible for his sons to conquer Shechem before it was time for the Canaanites to be expelled.] After G-d promised Avraham the land (12:7), he moved from there, pitching his tent between Bethel and Ai (12:8), as a sign that Yehoshua would capture this place first.

Possibly the Torah mentions *the Canaanites were then in the land* to inform us that Avraham came to the land of Canaan, but G-d did not tell him this was the land promised to him. He traveled as far as Shechem, while the Canaanites—that brutal and foolish nation—occupied the land. Because Avraham was afraid of them; he did not build an altar to G-d. But when he came to the area of Shechem, to Elon Moreh, G-d appeared to him, giving him the land (12:7). Hearing this, he was no longer afraid, for G-d had already promised him, *Go to the land that I will show you . . . I will make your name great, and you shall be a blessing* (12:1). Undaunted, he built an altar to G-d to worship Him openly.

Avram's Call

12:8 From there, [Avram] moved on to the mountains east of Bethel. He set up his tent with Bethel to the west and Ai to the east. He built an altar there and called in the name of Hashem.

He called in the name of Hashem—Onkelos explains that he prayed there, similar to the verse, *I called on Your name, Hashem, from the depths of the pit* (*Eichah* 3:55).

The correct interpretation is that he proclaimed G-d's name in a loud voice, announcing G-d's name and His Divinity. In Ur Kasdim he taught the people though they would not listen. When he came to the land where G-d's promise of *I will bless those who bless you* would be fulfilled, he was used to teaching and promoting belief in G-d.

Yitzchak also went to *Nachal Gerar*, and G-d promised him, *Do not be afraid for I am with you*. Therefore he built an altar there and *called in Hashem's name* (26:24,25). [Like Avraham,] he came to a new place where they had never heard of G-d nor seen His glory, and He proclaimed His glory among these people. However, [the Torah does not tell us that] Yaakov [made G-d's name known], because he had many children, all of whom were devout servants of G-d, and he had a great community called "the assembly of Yisrael" (*Shemos* 12:3). Through them collectively, belief [in one G-d] was spread and became known to everyone. Besides, belief in G-d was already established throughout Canaan since the days of Yaakov's ancestors. Indeed, the Rabbis (*Bereishis Rabbah* 39:24) comment on the phrase, *He called in the name of Hashem*: This teaches us that he caused everyone to call out the name of G-d.

PREINDICATION OF THE EXODUS

12:10 There was a famine in the land. Avram headed south to Egypt to stay there for a while, since the famine had grown very severe in the land.

There was a famine in the land—Avraham went down to Egypt temporarily, to survive the drought, but the Egyptians persecuted him for no reason, taking away his wife. G-d retaliated by striking Pharaoh with severe plagues and taking Avraham out of Egypt with cattle, silver and gold. Pharaoh even provided an escort for him.

G-d thus hinted to Avraham, that his children would go down to Egypt because of famine, stay there temporarily, and the Egyptians would treat them heartlessly, taking their women, as it says, *every girl shall be allowed to live* (*Shemos* 1:22).[57] But G-d would strike back at them with great plagues, until finally taking *b'nei Yisrael* out [of Egypt] with silver and gold and a huge amount

---

[57] They allowed the girls to live in order to be used for immoral purposes (*Shemos Rabbah* 1:22).

of livestock, while the Egyptians urged them to leave the land. There was no detail that happened to the Patriarch (Avraham) that did not happen to the children.

AVRAHAM'S UNINTENTIONAL SIN

The Rabbis explain [why G-d afflicted Avraham]:[58] R. Pinchas said in the name of R. Oshaya: G-d said to Avraham: "Go forth and clear a path for your children."[59] Accordingly, whatever is written about Avraham is written about his children also. In connection with Avraham it says, *There was a famine in the land*; in connection with Yisrael it says, *There has been a famine in the land for two years* (45:6).

Unintentionally[60] Avraham committed a grave sin, placing his righteous wife at risk of sin because he was afraid of being killed. He should have trusted in G-d to save him, his wife and all his belongings, for G-d has the power to help and save. He also sinned by leaving the country of his destiny, because of famine. G-d would have saved him from starvation. Because [he left Eretz Yisrael to go to Egypt], the exile in Egypt under the rule of Pharaoh was decreed for his children. In the place of punishment there was wickedness.

THE FOUR KINGDOMS

14:1 It happened in the days of Amrafel, king of Shinar; Arioch, king of Elasar; Kedorla'omer, king of Elam, and Tidal, king of Goyim.

---

[58] *Bereishis Rabbah* 40:8.
[59] Meaning: Carve a path of how to save yourself from the famine, so that your children will follow in this path. G-d decreed that there would be a famine in the land of Canaan in the days of his children. G-d wanted Avraham to prepare the best way to escape from the famine, hoping that Avraham would trust G-d and remain in Canaan. But Avraham took the wrong course, bringing great suffering on his children.
[60] Avraham thought that he had to do this to save his life.

It happened in the days of Amrafel—This event teaches us that four kingdoms [Babylonia, Persia, Greece, and Rome,] will arise who will rule the world. In time to come, Avraham's descendants will conquer them, and [the kingdoms] will fall into their hands. Then they will retrieve their captives and property.

The first of the four kings [mentioned in the verse] was the king of Babylonia,[61] and so it will be in the future, as [Daniel said to the king of Babylonia,] *You are the head of gold* (*Daniel* 2:34). Perhaps Elasar [the second kingdom mentioned in the verse] was the name of a city in Media or Persia. Elam was the city where the first Greek king [Alexander] was crowned. From there [Alexander's] kingdom expanded when he defeated Darius [king of Persia]. The Gemara quotes Rabbi Yose: "For six years the Greeks reigned in Elam, and after that their kingdom spread over the world". [Tidal] was called the king of Goyim [i.e., king of Nations] because he ruled over many different nations who had appointed him as their leader. His title, King of Nations [means King of Rome], for he ruled over a city that took in many nationalities: Kittim, Edomites, and others.

This concept is mentioned in *Bereishis Rabbah* 42:2: R. Avin says: Just as [Avraham's distress] began with the war of the four kingdoms, so will it end [with his children suffering under the] four kingdoms, [Babylonia, Persia, Greece, and Rome]. Furthermore it says: *It happened in the days of Amrafel king of Shinar*—this is Babylonia; *Arioch king of Elasar*—this is Media (Persia); *Kedorla'omer, king Elam*—this is Greece; *and Tidal, king of Goyim*—this is the kingdom of Edom (Rome) which is the dominant superpower.

THE MIRACULOUS RESCUE OF THE KING OF SEDOM

14:10 Siddim Valley was full of mud pits, and when the kings of Sedom and Amorah tried to flee, they fell into them. The others fled to the mountains.

---

[61] Shinar is Babylonia, as Onkelos translates it.

Full of mud pits—Rashi explains: There were many pits, because they dug up earth to use as mortar in construction projects. The Midrash says the mud [in the pits] was spongy, and only by a miracle did the king of Sedom escape. This miracle was performed for the people who did not believe that Avram was rescued from the fiery furnace in Ur Kasdim. When [the king of Sedom miraculously] escaped from the mud pit, they reconsidered and believed in Avram's [miraculous rescue. End of Rashi's commentary].

There is no doubt that the verse should be translated as mud pits, [and the kings sank into the mud]. The pits were similar to the one in which Yirmeyah was thrown, as it says, *In the pit there was no water, only mud, and Yirmeyah sank [partially] into the mud* (*Yirmeyah* 38:6). And it says, *He raised me from the pit of raging waters, from the slimy mud* (*Tehillim* 40:3). It is possible [to interpret that the king of Sedom] climbed out of the pit by himself, without a miracle.

I question the interpretation of the Midrash [which says it was a miraculous escape], for those who did not believe G-d made a miracle for Avraham, would not be convinced after seeing a miracle for the king of Sedom. The king of Sedom was an idol worshipper, and his miraculous escape would bolster their pagan beliefs, or cause them to believe that miracles are done by witchcraft or are a fluke of nature. In fact, the miracle of the king of Sedom might raise doubts to those who did believe in Avraham's miracle!

Perhaps the Rabbis [of the above-mentioned Midrash] interpret the verse, *The king of Sedom came out to meet [Avraham]* (14:17), to mean, he came out of the pit miraculously when Avraham passed by, in honor of Avraham, to meet and bless him. Or perhaps, upon his return from the battle, Avraham looked into the pit to save the kings [of Sedom and Amorah] wishing to return their property to them. It was then that the king of Sedom miraculously escaped from the pit. When the people saw a miracle happen to the king of Sedom in honor of Avraham, they concluded that surely a miracle was performed for Avraham himself, saving his life [from the fiery furnace].

YERUSHALAYIM, CITY OF RIGHTEOUSNESS

14:18 Malkitzedek king of Shalem brought forth bread and wine. He was a priest to G-d, the Most High.

Malkitzedek king of Shalem—*Shalem* is Yerushalayim, as it says, *His Tabernacle was in Shalem and His dwelling in Tzion* (*Tehillim* 76:3). Another proof that we are dealing with Yerushalayim is that it's king was called Malki-zedek, the king of "righteous" and in the days of Yehoshua, the king of Yerushalayim was called Adoni-zedek. Since the dawn of history, people knew that this place, situated in the center of the inhabited part of the world, was the best. Perhaps they knew by tradition, that it is exactly opposite the heavenly Beis Hamikdash where the *Shechinah* of The Holy One, blessed be He, who is called *Tzedek* (the Righteous One) dwells.

In *Bereishis Rabbah* 43:6 [we learn that Yerushalayim is called *Tzedek* because] "this place makes its inhabitants righteous," as it says, *Tzedek (righteousness) lodged in it* (*Yeshayah* 1:21). Malkitzedek means "the King of Tzedek" and Adonizedek means "the master of Tzedek."

MALKITZEDEK

He was a priest to G-d, the Most High—Avraham would not give tithe to a priest of other gods, but since he knew Malkitzedek *was priest to G-d, the Most High*, he gave him the tithe in honor of G-d (14:20). Avraham's encounter with Malkitzedek foreshadowed future times when the House of G-d will be in Yerushalayim, where his descendants will bring the tithe and *terumah* offerings, and bless Hashem.

According to the view of the Rabbis who say Malkitzedek was Shem, the son of Noach, we must explain that he left his country and went to Yerushalayim to worship Hashem. The Canaanites [who lived there] appointed him as priest of G-d the Most High, since [Shem] was the most respected of their father Cham's brothers. For Yerushalayim was always in the territory of the Canaanites.

He was a priest to G-d, the Most High—There were priests among the nations who worshipped angels called *eilim* (the mighty ones), as it says, *Who is like you* ba'eilim *among the heavenly powers* (*Shemos* 15:11), therefore, the Holy One, blessed be He, is called *G-d, the Most High*, meaning, "the Powerful One, the Highest of the High."[62]

WHY AVRAHAM ASKED FOR G-D'S ASSURANCE

15:2 Avram said, "O Hashem, G-d, what can You give me, if I remain childless? The heir to my household will be Damesek Eliezer."

Avram said, "O Hashem, G-d, what can You give me"—[As if to say:] "Look, You have saved me from the kings, but You have not promised me I will not die childless. You promised me *great reward* (15:1), but of what value is my reward without children?"

Avraham knew that the great reward promised to him, was not referring to the World to Come, regarding this there is no need for a promise, since every servant of G-d is fully assured of life in the World to Come. By contrast reward in this world requires affirmation, because there are righteous men whose portion in this world is [as harsh] as if they had sinned [like] the wicked. For this reason the righteous need assurance.

Additionally the promise of *great reward* (15:1) implies that he would merit both worlds, receiving all the good without any punishment, as befits the truly righteous.

Moreover an assurance is given for something one fears, [since

---

[62] The Canaanites who worshipped angels believed that there is a Supreme Being who rules the angels, and Malkitzedek was the priest of this Supreme Power.

Avraham feared remaining childless in this world; G-d] repeated the promise, explaining that he need not be afraid, since He would make his offspring as numerous as the stars of the sky.

THERE IS NO ASSURANCE FOR THE RIGHTEOUS

G-d had already told Avraham, *For all the land that you see, I will give to you and to your offspring forever. I will make your offspring like the dust of the earth* (13:15,16). How could Avraham say, *If I remain childless . . . a member of my household will inherit what is mine* (15:2,3)? Besides if he did not believe the first prophecy, why would he believe the prophecy G-d [revealed to him in the verses that follow]? The answer is, that the righteous do not believe in their virtue, fearing that perhaps they may have sinned inadvertently, as it says, *Or, one moment I may speak concerning a nation or a kingdom, to build and establish it, but if they do what is wrong in My eyes, not heeding My voice, then I relent of the goodness that I had said to bestow on it* (*Yirmeyah* 18:9). When Avraham saw himself growing old with the first prophecy [of children] unfulfilled, he feared that through his sins he had forfeited the good things [he was promised]. And perhaps he also feared he would be punished for killing people in the war, as the Rabbis have said. Similarly, they explain the verse about Yaakov, *Yaakov became very frightened, and it distressed him* (32:8), stating: From here we derive that there is no assurance for the righteous in this world . . ."

HE COUNTED IT AS RIGHTEOUSNESS

15:6 [Avram] believed in Hashem, and He counted it as righteousness—Rashi explains the verse: The Holy One, blessed be He, counted Abraham's belief in Him for merit and for righteousness.

RAMBAN'S INTERPRETATION:

[But the Ramban asks:] I do not understand why this should be counted as a merit for Avraham. Why shouldn't Abraham, a prophet, believe in the trustworthiness of G-d, since God is not human that He should be false. Wouldn't one whose faith was so strong he was ready to sacrifice his only beloved son, and withstand other tests, believe this good tiding?

It seems to me that the correct interpretation is [since Hashem now promised him children unconditionally he realized the promise was based on Hashem's righteousness, not his own merit for] originally G-d had told him, *Your reward will be great*, [and reward may be canceled through sin], but now he believed, because of G-d's righteousness, he would be granted a child, no matter what. Now he was no longer afraid that sin might cause the promised reward to be canceled.[63] The first promise was given as a reward for his deeds, but now that G-d told him to be unafraid of sin, promising a child, he believed the matter was settled, and G-d would not renege. G-d would do it out of His righteousness which is steadfast and unalterable, as it says, *I swear by Myself, righteousness has gone forth from My mouth, a word that will not be rescinded* (*Yeshayah* 45:23).

RAMBAN'S ALTERNATIVE INTERPRETATION

Alternatively, the verse may be telling us that Avraham believed he would unconditionally have a son as an heir. G-d considered this promise an act of righteousness, meaning, G-d made the promise out of G-d's righteousness.[64] [The phrase *He counted it as righteous* is understood] as the verse, *G-d considered it for good* (50:20), and the verse about Pinchas, *It was considered to him as a righteous deed, for all generations* (*Tehillim* 106:31). The faith Pinchas had in G-d when he did that particular deed[65] was considered as righteousness

---

[63] Thus, according to Ramban, it was Avraham who considered it Hashem's righteousness that He would give him children.

[64] Thus, G-d considered His promise of a son as an act of righteousness that will endure forever.

[65] See *Bamidbar* 25:7,8.

for all time. Because of Pinchas' deed, G-d will forever keep for him His righteousness and kindness, as it says, *Forever shall I keep My kindness for him* (*Tehillim* 89:29).

ABRAHAM'S CRUCIAL QUESTION

15:7,8 Hashem said to him, "I am Hashem who took you out of Ur Kasdim to give you this land as a possession. And he [Avraham] asked "How will I know that I will inherit it"?

I am Hashem who took you out of Ur Kasdim . . . I have already explained[66] this verse to mean: When I brought you out of Ur Kasdim, performing a miracle for you [by saving you from the fiery furnace] it was My will to give you this land. But He did not decree to give it to Abraham [unconditionally]; instead, He said He brought him out of Ur Kasdim with the intention of giving the land to him. Although G-d had told Avraham twice, *I will give this land to your offspring* (12:7 and 13:15), Avrohom worried that the inheritance of the land was dependent on deeds [and only if he and his offspring were totally righteous, would they acquire it], for G-d had not decreed unconditionally to give him the land as He did with a child. Therefore he asked, How can I really know that I am to inherit it?

Avrohom was not asking for a sign as did Chizkiyah who asked, *What sign [can you show me] that Hashem will heal me?* (2 *Melachim* 20:8). And G-d did not give him a sign as He did with others. Avraham only wished to know clearly that he would indeed inherit the land, without his or his offspring's sin denying it to them. Or perhaps the Canaanites might repent, in which case G-d would deal with them according to the verse, *One moment I may speak concerning a nation or a kingdom, to destroy, demolish or an-*

---

[66] in the commentary on 11:28.

nihilate it, but if that nation repents of its evil deed of which I had spoken, then I relent of the evil [decree] that I had planned to carry out against it (*Yirmeyah* 18:7,8). Therefore G-d responded with a covenant that he will inherit the land, come what may.

WHY THE EGYPTIANS WERE PUNISHED

15:14 But also the nation to which they are enslaved, I will bring judgment on them, and afterwards they will go free with great wealth.

But also the nation to which they are enslaved—Rashi explains that the word "also", includes the four kingdoms[67] of the four exiles which will [also] be punished for enslaving Yisrael.

According to the plain meaning of the verse, G-d says: Just as I decreed exile and affliction for your children because of [Avraham's] sin,[68] so will I judge the nation that enslaves them for the violence they will inflict on them. They will not be able to [claim immunity] saying they carried out My decree [that Avraham's descendants be oppressed].

Thus, the correct meaning of "also" is "even though, nevertheless." G-d said: "Even though I decreed your children will be foreigners in a land that is not theirs, enslaved and oppressed, nevertheless, I will judge the nation that will enslave them for what they will do, and they will not be absolved for having carried out My decree."

[They deserve to be punished] because [they oppressed the Jews ruthlessly,] as it says, *I have become zealous for Yerushalayim and for Tzion; and I am very angry with those nations that are at ease, for I was only angry a little, but they overdid the punishment* (*Zechariah* 1:14,15), and, *I was angry at My people, I defiled My heritage; I put them in your hands, but you showed them no mercy. Even upon the aged you made your yoke exceedingly heavy* (*Yeshayah* 47:6).

---

67 Babylonia, Persia, Greece, and Rome.
68 For leaving Eretz Yisrael and going to Egypt; see Ramban on verse 12:10.

That is what happened in Egypt. They oppressed them with undue harshness, throwing Jewish children into the river, making their lives miserable, and planning to wipe out every trace of them. This is the meaning of the phrase, *I will bring judgment on them*— to determine whether they tormented Yisrael as was decreed, or to excess.[69] This is what Yisro had in mind when he said, *for in the very matter in which [the Egyptians] overstepped their rights against [the Jews]* (*Shemos* 18:11). Their presumptuousness caused the Egyptians to be wiped out completely. And so it says, *You performed signs and wonders against Pharaoh, all his servants, and all the people of his land. For You knew that they sinned flagrantly against them* (*Nechemiah* 9:10).

THE RAMBAN DIFFERS WITH THE RAMBAM'S ANSWER

The Rambam in *Sefer Hamadda*[70] writes: [The Egyptians were punished though G-d had decreed they were to oppress the Jews, because] G-d did not order any particular Egyptian to harm the Jews. Each individual Egyptian who abused a Jew had the option not to do so.

I cannot accept his reasoning. If G-d decreed that any non-Jew harm the Jews, and an individual was quick to carry out G-d's decree, he would be doing a mitzvah. How could [the Rambam say] this person should be punished? If a king orders his subjects to do something, a lazy man who lets others do his share of the work breaks the law and infuriates the king, while one who does the work pleases the king. Surely in this case, no Egyptian could avoid doing his duty, since G-d had said, *But also the nation to which they*

---

[69] One may ask: Although the Egyptians went to extremes in oppressing the Jews, they should be punished only for the excessive oppression, not for the oppression itself. The answer is: By inflicting unreasonable pain on the Jews, the Egyptians showed that they did not mean to do G-d's will, but that they acted purely out of hatred and viciousness (*Kedushas Levi*).

[70] *Hilchos Teshuvah* 6:5.

are enslaved, clearly implying that the entire Egyptian nation would enslave them, and the Jews came to Egypt voluntarily [so that the Egyptians didn't even have to chase them]. Rather [the Egyptians deserved to be punished] because they oppressed the Jews excessively as I have written above.

In *Shemos Rabbah* (30:15), our Rabbis explain this with the following analogy: [In a fit of anger] a ruler decreed that his son work, stipulating that it be without harassment. The son went to work, but his employer refused to pay him, and hounded him day and night. When the ruler reconciled with his son, he condemned to death those who had mistreated the prince. The same way, the Holy One, blessed be He, decreed *b'nei Yisrael* be enslaved in Egypt. But the Egyptians brutally tyrannized them. Said the Holy One, blessed be He: You should have treated them as servants who take care of your needs. *I was only angry a little, but they overdid the punishment* (*Zechariah* 1:15).

[Although G-d decreed that the Egyptians enslave and oppress the Jews] throwing the Jewish children into the river was not included in the decree of, *They will be enslaved and oppressed* (15:13), for this would mean their total destruction. The Egyptians also added, *Come, let us outsmart them, lest they become numerous* (*Shemos* 1:10), which is not included in servitude or oppression. Besides, the Egyptians increased the affliction, as it says, *They embittered their lives with harsh servitude* (*Shemos* 1:14). Thus the Torah says, *[G-d] saw our suffering, our harsh labor, and our [excessive] oppression* (*Devarim* 26:7).

THE EGYPTIANS WERE DRIVEN BY BURNING HATRED

If someone was inscribed and sealed on Rosh Hashanah, to be killed [during the upcoming year], the bandit who kills him cannot claim immunity because he carried out the death sentence. Although this wicked man died for his crime, his blood will be avenged on the murderer. However, if someone heard this death sentence from a prophet, and therefore killed the offender, G-d will judge his act according to his intention. If his intention was to carry out G-d's will, then he is commended for killing him, as was the case with King Yeihu, who was rewarded by G-d for killing the house of Achav, as it says, *Because you have done well, doing that which is proper in My eyes, for you have done to the house of Achav according to all that was in My heart, four generations of your descendants will sit on the throne of Yisrael for your sake* (2 *Melachim* 10:30). But if he killed him out of hatred, or to take his wealth, he will be punished, since his intention was to sin, and his act is a transgression.

WHY SANCHERIV, KING OF ASSYRIA, WAS PUNISHED

Thus, the prophet Yeshayah spoke about Sancheriv [king of Assyria], *Woe to Assyria, rod of My anger; My wrath is a staff in their hand. Against a hypocritical people [Yisrael] shall I send them, and against a people that angers Me shall I charge them, to take spoils and to make them trampled like the mire in the streets. But he does not imagine this, and his heart does not think this way; for his heart is set to destroy, and to cut off nations, without leaving anything* (*Yeshayah* 10:5-7). Therefore Sancheriv was ultimately punished, as it says, *But it will be that after the Lord completes all His work, at Mount Tzion and Yerushalayim, I will deal with the fruits of the Assyrian king's conceit, and with the glory of his arrogant eyes* (10:12).[71] And Yirmeyah said this about Sancheriv, *Yisrael is like scattered sheep—lions have dispersed them; the first one, the king of Assyria, devoured him, and this last one, Nevuchadnetzar king of Babylonia, chewed up the bones. Therefore, thus said Hashem . . .*

---

[71] You may ask: The verse says that G-d punishes Assyria for their arrogance, but not for the destruction they brought on Yisrael. Therefore the Ramban continues by quoting the verse from Yirmeyah, showing that he was punished because he vandalized Yisrael out of arrogance in order to expand his kingdom, not to fulfill the will of G-d.

Behold I will punish the king of Babylon and his land as I have pun-ished the king of Assyria (*Yirmeyah* 50:17,18). This proves the king of Assyria was punished because of the evil he did to Yisrael.[72]

WHY NEVUCHADNETZAR WAS PUNISHED

Consider Nevuchadnetzar; he heard the prophets call on him to destroy Yerushalayim, as it says, *Behold, I am sending and will take all the families of the North—the word of Hashem—and [am sending] to Nevuchadnetzar king of Babylonia, My servant; and I shall bring them upon this land, and upon its inhabitants . . . and I shall destroy them* (*Yirmeyah* 25:9). Then it says, *Behold, I am de-livering this city into the hand of the Chaldeans who are attacking it and into the hand of Nevuchadnetzar king of Babylonia and he will capture it . . . and set the city on fire* (*Yirmeyah* 32:28,29). Concerning the Beis Hamikdash itself, the prophet said, *So I shall make this house like Shiloh* (*Yirmeyah* 26:6).[73] The Babylonians knew they were fulfilling G-d's command, as Nevuzaradan said to Yirmeyah, *Hashem your G-d threatened this place with disaster; and now Hashem has brought it about. He has acted as He threatened be-cause you sinned against Hashem* (*Yirmeyah* 40:2,3). Yet despite this, the Babylonians were punished for two reasons. Firstly, Nevuchadnetzar planned to destroy the whole land in order to ex-pand his empire, as it says, *I will end the pride of the wanton and bring low the haughtiness of the mighty* (*Yeshayah* 13:11), and, *Once you thought in your heart, I will climb to the sky; higher than the stars of G-d I will set my throne. . . I will mount the back of a cloud; I will liken myself to the Most High* (*Yeshayah* 14:13); and, *Who thinks to*

---

[72] You may ask: Perhaps Sancheriv was punished because he did not hear the prophetic decree and came on his own accord, but the Egyptians who did hear the decree that Yisrael was to be enslaved, why were they punished? Therefore the Ramban relates that Nevuchadnetzar who did hear the prophecies of several prophets was punished because he, like the other oppressors, harmed Yisrael in order to enlarge their territory, but not in order to do G-d's will.

[73] The *mishkan* at Shiloh was destroyed by the Philistines (1 Shmuel *4:10,11*).

himself, *"I am, and there is none but me"* (*Yeshayah* 47:8); and,
Chavakuk said about Nevuchadnetzar, *Woe to him who gains evil
profit for his house, so that he may set his nest up high* (*Chavakuk* 2:9).
The prophet equates Nevuchadnetzar with Sancheriv and they
were punished for the same reason as it says, *Therefore, thus said
Hashem . . . I will punish the king of Babylonia and his land just as
I punished the king of Assyria* (*Yirmeyah* 50:18).

Secondly, the king of Babylonia was punished, because he in-
flicted hardship on the Jews far more brutal than G-d had dictated.
And so it says about him, *I became angry at My people; I degraded
My heritage and delivered them into your hand. You showed them no
compassion; you made your yoke very heavy on the aged* (*Yeshayah*
47:6). Therefore, [Nevuchadnetzar] was stricken with a double
punishment: his people were completely wiped out, as it says, *I will
wipe out from Babylonia, name and remnant, child and grandchild*
(*Yeshayah* 14:22), and his city was destroyed forever, as it says, *And
Babylonia, glory of kingdoms, proud splendor of the Chaldeans shall
become like G-d's overturning of Sedom and Amorah . . . Nevermore
shall it be settled nor dwelled in throughout the ages . . . Owls will live
there, and demons will dance there* (*Yeshayah* 13:19-21). A further
verse states, *For it is the vengeance of Hashem, vengeance for His
Sanctuary* (*Yirmeyah* 51:11), and, *"May the violence done against
me and my kin be upon Babylonia,"* says the inhabitant of Tzion;
"and let my blood be upon the inhabitants of Chaldea" says
*Yerushalayim. Therefore, thus says Hashem: Behold, I take up your
grievance and take vengeance for you* (*Yirmeyah* 51:35,36). There
are many more verses like these.

THREE PROMISES

15:18 On that day, Hashem made a covenant with
Avram, saying, "To your descendants I have given
this land, from the Egyptian River as far as the great river, the
Euphrates . . ."

On that day, Hashem made a covenant with Avram, saying—
G-d promised Avraham the land many times, and each promise was
made for a specific purpose. When he arrived in the land for the
first time, G-d promised him, *I will give this land to your offspring*
(12:7)[informing him that this was his destination], without de-
tailing its boundaries, because the phrase *this land* refers only to the
land he had passed through on his way to the area of Shechem,
coming to the Plain of Moreh.

Afterwards, when his merits increased, G-d added [a second
promise], *Raise your eyes, and, from the place where you are now
[standing], look to the north, to the south, to the east, and to the west.
For all the land that you see, I will give to you and your offspring forever* (13:14,15). This time G-d pledged to give him those lands.
The phrase, *that you see* does not mean only what one actually sees
with one's eyes, for that is not very far. Rather G-d will give him
the land that extends in each direction he looks. Or it may be that
He miraculously showed him all of Eretz Yisrael, as He did with
Moshe Rabbeinu (*Devarim* 34:1-3). G-d added that He will give
the land to his offspring forever, and make his offspring like the
dust of the earth in this second promise.

In the third promise, at the Covenant of the Halves, G-d de-
tailed the boundaries of the land, mentioning the ten nations [liv-
ing there at the time.] In addition, He made a covenant with
Avrohom that his descendants inherit the land forever. Even if they
sinned, the promise would not be canceled.

At the time G-d commanded Avraham about circumcision, He
told him the land was an *eternal heritage* (17:8), meaning, if his descendants were exiled, they would return to take possession of it
again. He added, *I will be a G-d to you and to your offspring* (17:7),
meaning that He in His glory will lead them, and their destiny
would not be determined by a star, a constellation, or a spiritual
power, as will be explained.[74]

G-d used the future tense, for the first and second promises: *To*

74 In *Vayikra* 18:25, *Devarim* 4:15, and 29:25.

your offspring I will give this land (12:7), and *I will give to you*
(13:15), because the gift was not yet complete for He had not
given him the entire land. But the third time, at the Covenant of
the Halves, He said, *To your descendants I have given the land*
(15:18) in the past tense, informing Avrohom He is making the
covenant for the gift He had already given him. When G-d commanded him about the circumcision, mentioning, *for an eternal
heritage,* He also used the future tense, *To you and your offspring I
will give the land* (17:8).[75]

Rashi explains [that the past tense, is used] because a promise of
the Holy One, blessed be He, is considered done already. But there
is no need to explain it this way.

THE PUNISHMENT FOR TREATING HAGAR BADLY

16:6 Avram replied to Sarai, "Your slave is in your hands.
Do with her as you see fit." Sarai treated her harshly, and [Hagar] ran away from her.

Sarai treated her harshly—Our mother Sarah erred by treating
her harshly, and Avraham also transgressed by permitting her to do
so. Therefore G-d heard Hagar's prayer, giving her a son who
would be a wild man afflicting the descendants of Avraham and
Sarah with untold afflictions.

A SIGN FOR THE FUTURE

16:9 The angel of G-d said to [Hagar], "Return to your
mistress, and submit yourself to her."

---

[75] For this was a promise for the future, that if they were to be exiled, they would
return and inherit it again, as the Ramban explained in the previous paragraph.

Return to your mistress, and submit yourself to her—The angel commanded this return, indicating that in the future she will not be free, rather, Sarah's children will forever rule over her children.

THE DIVINE NAME SHA-DAI

17:1 Avram was 99 years old. G-d appeared to him and said, "I am *E-l Sha-dai* (G-d Al-mighty) Walk before Me and be perfect.

E-l Sha-dai—Each of these Names stands for a different Divine Attribute. *E-l* means "powerful," as in, *Trembling gripped the powers of Moav* (*Shemos* 15:15). According to Rashi, the name *Sha-dai* [is a contraction of the words "there is" and "sufficient"] describing G-d as the one "Who has sufficient power to give what is necessary." The Rambam, *Moreh Nevuchim* (1:63) explains that *Sha-dai* means "He Who is sufficient," that is, He does not require any other being to complete the existence of the things He created, or to keep them intact; His existence alone is sufficient.[76]

Rabbi Avraham ibn Ezra, quoting Rabbi Shmuel Hanagid, explains that *Sha-dai* is related to the word *shodeid*, "to overpower." Thus the name *Sha-dai* means, "He who controls and dominates the heavenly hosts." This is the correct interpretation, for the name *Sha-dai* stands for the Attribute of Power by which G-d runs the world. The Sages call it "the Attribute of Justice of the world below."

---

[76] G-d revealed to Avraham His name *Sha-dai*, "He who is sufficient" so that he should not think that He needs Avraham to walk before Him and be perfect, in order to preserve and maintain the world that G-d created.

HIDDEN AND OPEN MIRACLES

The name *Sha-dai,* is appropriate here because with this name the hidden miracles[77] are performed for the righteous, to rescue their soul from death, and to sustain them in famine, and to save them from being killed in war, like the miracles that were done for Avraham and the other Patriarchs, and like the blessings and curses mentioned [in the *Tochachah*] in *parashas Bechukosai* and *parashas Ki Savo.* These blessings and curses are miracles, because it is not natural for rains to fall when we serve G-d, or that the skies be like iron if we plant our fields in the seventh year.[78] Similarly, all promises in the Torah whereby the natural order is overpowered without causing noticeable change in the normal scheme of things are miracles [using the name Shadai]. However the miracles done by Moshe Rabbeinu—such as the ten plagues, the parting of the sea, the manna, the well—as well as others, were open miracles whereby nature was changed for all to see. They were performed with the Four-Letter Divine name, which G-d had told him.

Therefore G-d now told Avraham, that He is the Almighty, the One who prevails and can overcome the signs of the stars [that predict he will be childless]. He will indeed have a son and there will be an everlasting covenant between Him and his offspring, meaning Hashem's portion is His people, and He Himself will lead them, not by a star, a constellation, or planetary influences.

Walk before Me—Means, follow the path which I will show you. It is similar to the command, *Walk after Hashem, your G-d, and remain in awe of Him* (*Devarim* 13:5). G-d says *Walk before me* when He tells someone to follow in His ways before giving specific instructions. When He tells one to follow in His ways after giving specific instructions, He says, *Walk after Hashem.* The meaning of

---

[77] Hidden miracles seem to be natural events, but in reality they come about by G-d guiding the forces of nature to achieve the desired result.
[78] The sabbatical year, when it is forbidden to plant and to harvest crops (*Vayikra* 25:1-7).

both commands is to fear Him alone, doing whatever He commands.

REJECT BELIEF IN ASTROLOGICAL SIGNS

Be perfect—This is an additional commandment similar to the command, *You must remain totally faithful to Hashem your G-d* (*Devarim* 18:13) which follows G-d's warning, *Among you, there shall not be found anyone . . . who practices divination, an astrologer, one who reads omens, a sorcerer . . .* (*Devarim* 18:10). One must believe wholeheartedly that the Holy One, blessed be He, alone, is the Almighty from beginning to end, and only He has the power to create and to destroy [in a supernatural way]. Therefore, scorn sorcerers and fortune-tellers, and know their words will not be fulfilled in any way, shape or form. Everything is in the hand of the One Above, the Almighty, *Sha-dai,* who does good to a person, even if his stars predict otherwise, and who brings evil on a person, even if his stars indicate good fortune. Based on a person behavior, He abrogates the omens of the stargazers and makes fools of astrologers. The Sages had this in mind when they said: [G-d told Avraham:] "Cast aside your astrological speculations" [meaning, abandon your belief in the influence of the stars].

Rashi explains *Be perfect,* "Be perfect, and withstand all the tests I will give you." Rabbi Avraham ibn Ezra says *Be perfect* means do not ask the reason for the mitzvah of *milah.* In his view, the word "perfect" is similar to the verse, *May my heart be perfect in Your statutes (Tehillim* 119:80). The correct interpretation is as I have explained, [reject all astrological calculations, believing wholeheartedly in the power of G-d to determine one's fate]. This idea is expressed in the verse, *May my heart be perfect in Your statutes, so that I not be shamed* (*Tehillim* 119:80).

ויראא

VAYEIRA

—◉—

THE THREE VISITORS

18:1,2 G-d appeared to [Avraham] in the Plains of Mamre while he was sitting at the entrance of the tent in the hottest part of the day. [Abraham] lifted his eyes and saw three men standing a short distance from him. When he saw them from the entrance of his tent, he ran to greet them, bowing down to the ground.

G-d appeared [to Avraham]—Rashi explains: To visit the sick [Avraham]. R. Chama b. R. Chanina said: It was the third day after his circumcision, and the Holy One, blessed be He, came to inquire after Abraham's health.

He saw three men—[The three men] who came to him were angels in the form of men.

Three—One came to announce [the birth of Yitzchak] to Sarah, one came to heal Avraham, and one came to destroy Sedom. [Three angels were needed, because an angel does not do more than one assignment.] The angel Refael who healed Avraham also rescued Lot, because being in a different place for a second mission, [constitutes a new assignment]. Or perhaps, because both assignments [healing and rescuing], have the same purpose [of saving lives], they are considered one assignment. [End of Rashi]

THE RAMBAM'S VIEW

The Rambam, *Moreh Nevuchim* (2:42), says [the phrase *G-d appeared to him* at the beginning of] this chapter tells us G-d appeared to Avraham in a prophetic vision. The verses continue with the details of this vision, describing that Avraham lifted his eyes and saw three men standing a short distance from him, and he said, *My lord, if I find favor in your eyes* (18:3). In his vision, he saw that he was speaking to their leader.

VISION OF ANGELS

[The Rambam's explanation, that the passage *G-d appeared to him,* means he had a prophecy of a vision of angels is difficult to accept]. If all that happened to Avraham when Hashem appeared to him was that he had a vision of men eating a meal, how can the verse say, *G-d appeared to him;* according to the Rambam—G-d did not appear to him, in vision or in thought? Besides, the phrase [*G-d appeared to him*] never occurs in connection with prophecy.

[Additionally] following the Rambam's view, Sarah did not actually knead cakes, Avraham did not prepare a calf, and Sarah did not laugh to herself, for these were all only a vision! Why would G-d show him all these extraneous details in a vision [announcing the birth of a son]?

The Rambam in [*Moreh Nevuchim*] remarks similarly concerning the verse, *A man wrestled with him [Yaakov]* (32:25), explaining that episode as a prophetic vision. Yet, if so, I do not understand how Yaakov limped when he awoke. And why did he say, *For I have seen the Divine face to face, yet my life was spared* (32:31). Prophets are not afraid they will die after seeing prophetic visions. Besides, Yaakov had seen a greater and more exalted vision than this [in his dream of the ladder reaching into heaven]. In fact, in many prophetic visions he saw the glory of G-d.[79]

---

[79] *Bereishis* 28:13 and 31:3.

[Moreover: If the visiting angels were visions, not living men], the angels who visited Lot, did not actually come to his house, he did not bake matzos for them, and they did not eat. How is this possible? Even assuming that Lot reached the spiritual height of prophecy, how did the sinful people of Sedom become prophets? [If they were not prophets,] who told them men came into Lot's house?

And if these events were prophetic visions of Lot, then the rest of the story, where *the angels hurried Lot, saying, "Get moving. Take your wife and two daughters . . . Run for your life! . . . I will also give you special consideration"* (19:14-21) is also a vision, and Lot could have stayed in Sedom! [The Rambam] explains that the events took place, though the conversations in each episode were in a vision. But this flies in the face of the Torah text. It is forbidden to listen, much less, believe it!

DANIEL AND HAGAR SAW ANGELS BUT WERE NOT PROPHETS

It is true that seeing or hearing an angel can happen only in a vision or a dream, since human senses cannot perceive angels. But this is not a prophetic vision, since the level of seeing or hearing an angel is not a prophetic one. The Rambam is incorrect when he says[80], all prophets, except Moshe Rabbeinu, received prophecy through an angel. The Sages said: They [Chaggai, Zecharia, and Malachi] were superior to [Daniel] because they were prophets and he was not a prophet. Indeed, the Book of Daniel was not included in the books of the Prophets [but in the Book of the Writings], even though the angel Gavriel appeared and spoke to him while he was awake, as he says in his vision of the Second Beis Hamikdash, *I was still speaking in prayer, when the man Gavriel, whom I had seen in the earlier vision, was lifted in flight approaching me . . . and he*

---

80   *Moreh Nevuchim* 2:41 and *Hilchos Yesodei Hatorah* 7:6.

spoke to me (*Daniel* 9:21). He also had his vision about the ultimate redemption while awake, as he walked with his friends along the bank of the Tigris River.[81] Hagar, the Egyptian, is also not listed among the prophetesses,[82] [even though she saw an angel]. It is clear that she did not hear a *bas kol* [heavenly voice], as the Rambam contends[83] [but she heard an angel speak to her.]

The Torah differentiates between the prophecies of Moshe Rabbeinu and the Patriarchs, as it says, *I revealed Myself to Avraham, Yitzchak, and Yaakov as E-l Sha-dai—G-d Al-mighty* (*Shemos 6:3*). This name is one of the Creator's holy names, not the name of an angel, [thus G-d Himself appeared to the Fathers, speaking directly to them, not through an angel].

The Rabbis contrast the prophecies of Moshe Rabbeinu and other prophets, stating: "What is the difference between Moshe and all the prophets? All the prophets saw with blurred vision, as it says, *I spoke with the prophets and provided numerous visions, and through the prophets provided allegories* (*Hoshea* 12:11). But Moshe saw with clear vision, as it says, *He sees a true picture of G-d* (*Bamidbar* 12:8). This idea is mentioned in a number of places, but it never says the other prophets received their prophetic message through an angel.

Don't be misled by the verse, *I am also a prophet like you, and an angel spoke to me by the word of Hashem, saying* (1 *Melachim* 13:18) [which seems to indicate that the prophet received his message through an angel, supporting the Rambam's view]. Understand the verse as follows: *I also am a prophet, just as you are, and I know by prophecy that the angel who spoke to me conveyed a message from G-d.* This knowledge is one of the levels of prophecy, as the man of G-d said, *For thus has it been commanded to me [by an angel, and I know by prophecy that the decree is] by the word of Hashem* (1 *Melachim* 13:9), and then he said, *For a decree [has come] to me by the word of Hashem* (13:17).

---

[81]   *Daniel* 10:4.
[82]   The Gemara in *Megillah* 14a lists seven prophetesses.
[83]   *Moreh Nevuchim* 2:41.

Furthermore, the Sages comment on Bilam's address to the angle, *If you consider it wrong [for me to go], I will go back home* (*Bamidbar* 22:34), "I did not go [with Balak's emissaries] until the Holy One, blessed be He, told me, *Set out and go with them* (22:20), and you [an angel] tell me to return? G-d also told Avraham to sacrifice his son, and then, *an angel of Hashem called to him from heaven, and said . . . Do not harm the boy!* (*Bereishis* 22:11,12). He habitually says one thing, then sends an angel to take it back."

The Sages note that Avraham's first prophecy [commanding him to sacrifice his son] differs from the second prophecy [not to harm the boy] because the former mentions Hashem's name while the latter was conveyed through an angel. A prophet can receive a Divine command through prophecy, and that command may be canceled through an angel, since the prophet knows the angel spoke in G-d's name.

The Sages explain in *Vayikra Rabbah* (1:9): *G-d called to Moshe* (*Vayikra* 1:1); unlike the way He addressed Avraham. For we find, *G-d's angel called to Avraham a second time* (*Bereishis* 22:15); the angel called, but G-d spoke the word. Avraham attained prophecy only after he prepared himself spiritually to perceive an angel, rising from that level to the level of prophecy. However Moshe was ready to receive a prophetic message at all times, as G-d said: "I am the One who called, and I am the One who speaks."

SEEING AN ANGEL IS NOT PROPHECY

Thus the Sages teach us that seeing an angel is not prophecy, and people who see and speak with angels are not prophets, as I mentioned in connection with Daniel. Theirs is a vision called "uncovering the eyes," as in the verse, *Hashem uncovered Bilam's eyes, and he saw an angel of Hashem stationed in the way* (*Bamidbar* 22:31), and, *Elisha then prayed and said, "Hashem, please open his eyes that he may see!"*[84].

---

[84]   1 *Melachim* (6:17)

In this chapter, in the chapter about Lot, and in the verses, *A man [appeared and] wrestled with him* (*Bereishis* 32:25) and, *A man found [Yosef] blundering about in the fields* (37:15),[85] angels are called men. The Sages explain that when angels are called men, an ethereal spiritual light is created in angels, which the Kabbalists define as "a garment" that is visible to people with pure souls, such as the pious and students of prophets. I cannot explain it any further.

At times the Torah speaks of seeing G-d and hearing an angel speak, or seeing an angel and hearing G-d speak, for example, at the beginning Moshe Rabbeinu's prophecy (*Shemos* 3:2-4) and in Zechariah (3:1,2). Further on, I will reveal these words of the living G-d with mystical allusions.

Understand this chapter thusly: "*On the very day that Avraham was circumcised,* G-d appeared to him while he was still sick from his circumcision, as he sat at the entrance of his tent away from the heat. He was not prepared for a prophetic message, nor did he fall on his face or pray, and yet, he received this vision.

AVRAHAM'S VISION

The *Shechinah* appeared to Avraham [after he performed the milah] as a sign of honor and distinction like it appeared at the dedication of the Tabernacle, where it says, *Moshe and Aharon . . . came out and blessed the people. G-d's glory was then revealed to all the people* (*Vayikra* 9:23). Because they fulfilled the commandment of building the Tabernacle they merited seeing the *Shechinah*.

---

[85] The man who wrestled with Yaakov was the guardian angel of Eisav (*Bereishis Rabbah* 77:2); the man who found Yosef in the field was the angel Gavriel (*Tanchuma*, Vayeishev 2).

A Sign of Divine Approval

The appearance of the *Shechinah* at these times was not to instruct them about a mitzvah or inform them of something. Rather, it was a reward for doing a mitzvah, indicating that G-d approved of their deeds, as it says, *And I—in righteousness I shall behold your face; upon awakening I will be sated by Your image* (*Tehillim* 17:15).

Therefore, we find that Yaakov *encountered angels of G-d* (*Bereishis* 32:2), although they did not say anything or convey new ideas. He merited seeing angels of G-d, which assured him that G-d valued his deeds. Here too, the *Shechinah* appeared to Avraham implying that G-d approved his deed [of performing the circumcision].

The Midrash says: "At the Parting of the Sea, *b'nei Yisrael* marched forward, exclaiming, *This is my G-d, I will enshrine Him!* At that moment, a handmaid saw at the sea what Yechezkel the prophet never saw." This medrash means, in the merit of believing in G-d and His servant Moshe, they were worthy to behold the *Shechinah* at the time of the great miracle.

Sometimes the *Shechinah* appears in a moment of Divine anger to protect of His righteous servants and their honor. For example, *the whole community was threatening to stone [Moshe and Aharon] to death, when G-d's glory suddenly appeared in the Communion Tent before all Yisrael* (*Bamidbar* 14:10).

[If the *Shechinah* appeared to Avraham in the merit of *milah*, why are the vision of the *Shechinah* and the *milah* recorded in different sections in the Torah?] The second passage begins, *He appeared to him* rather than *G-d appeared to Avraham* implying a connection between the two incidents.

Here the Torah describes the honors bestowed on Avraham after he performed the circumcision. The *Shechinah* appeared to him, angels informed his wife [that she would give birth to a son], and Lot was saved because of him. G-d had already told Avraham he would have a son (17:19), but Sarah only found out now, overhearing the angel speaking to Avraham, as it says, *Sarah was listening behind the entrance to the tent* (18:10).

This is what the Sages meant when they said G-d appeared to Avraham "to inquire after his health," implying that the *Shechinah* came only to honor him, not to command or to inform him about anything.

The Midrash explains: It says, *Make an earthen altar for Me. . . Wherever I allow My name to be mentioned, I will come to you and bless you* (*Shemos* 20:21). If God will bless anyone who built an altar for His name, surely He will come and bless Avraham for circumcising himself for G-d's name.

[When the Sages said G-d appeared to Avraham to inquire after his health] they may have meant that the *Shechinah* would heal the *milah* also, as it says, *In the light of the King's countenance is life* (*Mishlei* 16:15).

G-D'S SPECIAL SUPERVISION OF THE RIGHTEOUS

18:19 For I have known him, because he commands his children and his household after him that they keep the way of Hashem, doing charity and justice . . .

For I have known him, because he commands—Rashi, like the Targum, defines the word "known" as an expression of love, as in *known through her husband* (*Ruth* 2:1), [which means a relative] and, *I have known you [intimately]* (*Shemos* 33:17). The primary meaning of "knowing" in these verses is love, because one who loves another seeks to know him well. You cannot translate the verse, *For I know that he will command his children*, for if so the word "because" is uncalled-for. [End of Rashi's commentary.]

The word *known* may mean, "I have raised him up and exalted him," as in, *I shall know you by name* (*Shemos* 33:12) [i.e., "I will make your name great"] and, *What is man, that you should know him?* (*Tehillim* 144:3) [i.e., that you have made him great. Thus we

interpret the verse:] "I shall make him a great and mighty nation, because he will command his children to do what is right before Me."

In my opinion, the simple translation of *known him* is correct,
for G-d uses only general supervision over the physical world,
watching over all species, including humans, through the laws of
nature. However, G-d exercises close supervision for G-d-fearing
people, watching them constantly. [Thus, *I have known him* is to be
understood as in the verse,] *He will not remove His eyes from a
righteous man* (*Iyov* 36:7), and, *Behold, the eye of Hashem is on those
who fear Him* (*Tehillim* 33:18), and many similar passages.

A Warning for B'nei Yisrael

[**G**-d destroyed Sodom because of its great wickedness. When
G-d sent angels in the form of men to Lot's house to save
him, the populace of Sedom demanded that these "men" be given
to them for immoral purpose.]

**And they [the people of Sedom] called to Lot, saying "Where
are the men who came to you for the night? Bring them out to
us and we will become intimate with them".**

19:5 That we may become intimate with them—Sedom
was judged because of the lofty level of Eretz Yisrael,
since Sedom is part of [Eretz Yisrael,] the "inheritance of Hashem"
which cannot tolerate people who engage in shameful perversions.
Just as the Land vomited out the [Canaanite] nation because of
their abominations, it vomited out [the people of Sedom] who be-
haved worse than all nations toward G-d and man. Because of their
prosperity, the people of Sedom were arrogant, therefore heaven
and earth became desolate, and the land was destroyed forever,
never to be revived.

G-d made them an example for all rebels in Yisrael who were
destined to inherit the land. He gave a similar warning with the

verse, *Sulphur and salt has burned all its soil . . . It is like the destruction of Sedom and Amorah, Admah and Tzevoyim, [the cities] that Hashem overturned in His anger and rage* (*Devarim* 29:22).

There were many sinful and wicked nations, yet G-d did not punish them as severely, proving that Sedom was punished because of the superiority of Eretz Yisrael, the site of the Sanctuary of Hashem.

THE ATROCITY IN GIVAH

[**In response to the demand of the populace Lot said:**] **(19:8) I have two daughters . . . I will bring them out to you. Do as you please with them, but don't do anything to these men . . .**

Although the episode of the concubine of Givah,[86] seems identical to the incident in Sedom, they are not comparable. The thugs in Givah did not intend to prevent travelers from entering their town [as the Sedomites did]. They were obsessed with immorality, wanting sexual relations with the Levite wayfarer; when he offered them his concubine, they were satisfied. The old man [who had invited the Levite into his house] said to the men of Givah, *Look, here is my virgin daughter and [the Levite's] concubine! Let me bring them out to you, and you may molest them and do to them whatever you please* (*Shofetim* 19:24), knowing they would not molest his daughter. And indeed they refused the offer of the daughter and were satisfied when offered the concubine. The Levite reasoned

---

[86] A man and his concubine wanted to spend the night in Givah. An old man took them into his house and gave them a meal. A band of depraved townspeople pounded on the door demanding to be intimate with the wayfarer. The old man tried to dissuade them, but when they would not listen, the wayfarer gave his concubine to them. They violated and abused her all night, and she died from the abuse. *Shofetim*, chapter 19.

Ramban digresses and explains at length how the episode in Givah, as horrifying and inexcusable as it was, is not comparable to the seemingly identical conduct of Sedom. In Givah, a lawless band of thugs terrorized the decent majority, but in Sedom, all elements of the city participated in the crime. In addition, in Sedom they did not act out of desire, rather their intent was to discourage wayfarers.

that since the concubine was not legally married[87] and had been unfaithful to him earlier, he could save himself this way.

Not all the townspeople in Givah, were involved in the rape, as it says, *Behold, people of the city, lawless people, surrounded the house* (19:22). They were the rulers and bullies of the city, as the Levite reported, *The lords of Givah rose up against me* (20:5), therefore no one protested. However, in Sedom, *The men of Sedom surrounded the house—young and old alike—all the people from every quarter* (19:4).

THE TRIBES WANT TO BRING THE EVILDOERS TO JUSTICE

[If the concubine, an unmarried woman who had previously been unfaithful, was abused by only a few ruffians, why did the tribes of Yisrael want to kill them?][88]

The leaders of all tribes in Yisrael wanted to kill them as an example [to prevent immorality], as it says, *Come, hand over those scoundrels in Giv'ah so that we may put them to death and stamp out the evil from Yisrael* (20:13). By Torah law, one is not liable to the death penalty for the crime of tormenting a concubine who is a harlot. They also did not intend murder, and in fact she did not die while with them, *for they let her go when dawn broke* (19:25). She died when she went back to her master's house, perhaps from exhaustion after the many sexual assaults and exposure, lying outside in front of the door all night.

Because the men of Giv'ah wanted to commit the same shameful act as the Sedomites, the tribes saw fit to "make a protective fence around the Torah" so this should never happen again, as it says, *Stamp out the evil from Yisrael* (20:13). Their judgment was based on the principle that the *Beis din* may impose lashes and pronounce capital sentences even when not warranted by the Torah; if they intend to protect the Torah, not disregard it.

---

[87] They were wrong, for it is forbidden to turn over one person to save another.
[88] When the Levite returned home, he called on all Yisrael to avenge her death.

The tribe of Binyamin [in whose territory Giv'ah was located] did not agree to [this death penalty], since legally they were not liable. Perhaps the people of Binyamin were also piqued, since the tribes made this decision without discussing the matter with them first.

BOTH BINYAMIN AND THE TRIBES ARE AT FAULT

In my opinion, the tribes of Yisrael were punished with defeat in the first battle because they did not fight according to Torah law. The tribe of Binyamin—not the tribes of Yisrael—should have "made a fence", since [the Sanhedrin of] each tribe is responsible for judging the people under its jurisdiction.

Both [Binyamin and Yisrael] deserved to be punished. Binyamin sinned, because they did not punish or reprimand the evildoers. Yisrael sinned by launching an unauthorized war. Even though they asked the Urim VeTumim who should lead the battle, they did not ask the word of Hashem if they should go to war. They made the decision to fight on their own. Similarly, relying on their superior manpower, they did not ask about the outcome of the battle, only asking, *Who among us should advance first to [wage] war against the children of Binyamin?* (*Shofetim* 20:18). Perhaps each tribe said, "I don't want to be first," or, "I want to be first." G-d answered them according to their question, *Yehudah should be first* (20:18), meaning: "Yehudah is always first," as it says, *For He chose Yehudah to be the ruler* (1 *Divrei Hayamim* 28:4), but He did not say: "Yehudah should go up," as in other places, because He did not give them permission [to go to war]. Yet, because the Binyaminites deserved to be punished, He did not stop them either telling them explicitly, "Do not go, and do not fight".

THE BINYAMINITES WIN

In this manner G-d removed His special supervision, leaving their fate to be determined by the uncertainties of nature. Since the

Binyaminites were gallant fighters living in fortified cities, they rout-
ed the tribes of Yisrael who relied on their military might [rather
than on trust in G-d]. However, the Binyaminites piled new sins on
top of old ones. Not content to chase Yisrael out of Giv'ah, they also
killed twenty-two thousand men, driven by deep-seated hatred.

After this defeat, the tribes of Yisrael realized they had erred in
attacking their brothers without receiving permission from G-d.
Therefore, on the second day they asked, *Shall we again join battle with the children of Binyamin, our brother?* (*Shofetim* 20:23), referring to Binyamin as their brother. G-d gave them permission to
avenge the death of their brothers, saying, *Go up against him*
(20:23). However, they did not ask whether they would win, for
they still relied on their greater numbers to bring them victory. G-d
only told them they were allowed to fight the Binyaminites, but did
not guarantee the outcome. Since their first sin had not yet been
atoned for, they lost another eighteen thousand men on the second
day.

HEAVY CASUALTIES ON BOTH SIDES

On the third day they decreed a fast, crying to G-d and offering burnt-offerings to atone for their sinful thoughts in relying on their military might. Considering themselves escapees from
the sword of Binyamin, they also offered thanksgiving peace offerings. As the law says, *Let them offer thanksgiving sacrifices, and tell
His deeds in joyful song* (*Tehillim* 107:22), and, *Now is my head high
over my enemies round-about; I offer in His tent with shouts of joy,
singing and chanting a hymn to Hashem* (*Tehillim* 27:6). The number of casualties among Yisrael during the two days of fighting was
40,000, while 25,000 fighters of Binyamin fell in battle, besides
those struck down in the populated cities. It is possible that the additional casualties among the [Benyaminite] men, women and children amounted to 15,000, thus making the punishment of the two
sides equal [both suffering 40,000 fatalities].

The Root Cause of the Disaster

How meaningful are the words of our Sages who said that the people of the concubine of Giv'ah were punished because of the idol of Michah.[89] For G-d said [to the people of that era]: "The insult to My honor [when Michah's idol was set up] you did not protest. While the offense to flesh and blood [i.e., the rape of the concubine at Giv'ah] you did protest. The sin of idol worship, deserves the death penalty and insults to My honor, yet you did not protest; the rape of the concubine is not a capital crime and involves the honor of a mortal yet you did protest." Therefore G-d confused both sides, making them stubborn and causing them to forget their brotherly bond.

Ultimately, they regretted their action, as it says, *The people came to Beis-El and sat before G-d until evening. They wailed and wept bitterly, and said, "O Hashem, G-d of Yisrael, why has this happened in Yisrael that one tribe must now be missing from Yisrael?"* (*Shofetim* 21:2). They recognized their mistake and punishment.

I have taken this opportunity to explain an obscure chapter, outlining the factors that caused [the events we described].

Why Lot Was Saved from Sedom

19:29 G-d remembered Avraham, and He allowed Lot to escape the upheaval—[What connection is there between G-d's remembering of Avraham and Lot?]

---

89   At the time of the Exodus, Moshe searched for Yosef's coffin in order to take it up to Eretz Yisrael. He heard that the Egyptians had sunk it in the Nile. Moshe then wrote the Divine name on a plate and cast it into the Nile, thereby raising the coffin. Michah stealthily retrieved this Divine Name from the Nile and used this Name to create an idol which he carried across the Red Sea and later built an idolatrous shrine for it (*Shofetim* ch. 18). Yet no one protested against this desecration. By contrast, when the concubine was violated and died, the tribes of Yisrael fought a bloody war to punish the perpetrators. Evidently they considered the crime against the concubine as a worse stain on their honor than the building of an idolatrous shrine.

Since Lot voluntarily accompanied Avraham in his wanderings, he deserved to be saved in his merit. Lot lived in Sedom only because of Avraham. Had he not accompanied Avraham, he would still be living with his family in Charan. It is impossible that any evil could happen to [Lot] because of Avraham who left Charan at G-d's command. For this reason too, Avraham risked his life, chasing after the kings[90] for [Lot's] sake.

WHY G-D TESTS THE RIGHTEOUS

22:1 **G-d tested Avraham**—[Why did the omniscient G-d Who knew in advance that Avraham would pass the test, test him?]

Since a person has total freedom to do or not do a deed, a difficult task is called a "test" from the perspective of the one being tested. G-d "tests" the person only to bring the potential good deed into actuality, to be able to reward him for the good deed, not just for the good intention.

Hashem only tests the righteous when He knows in advance that the *tzaddik* will do His will. He wants to make him even more righteous, by undergoing a test. He does not test the wicked who will not obey. All trials in the Torah are for the benefit of the one tested.

THE MANIFESTATION OF AVRAHAM'S FEAR OF G-D

22:12 **For now [that you passed this test] I know that you fear G-d**—[Didn't the omniscient G-d know this before?] At the beginning, Avraham's fear of G-d was dormant, not manifest by this great deed. But now his fear of G-d became known as an obvious reality. His merit was perfect, and his reward from G-d would be complete.

---

90   *Bereishis* 14:14.

PROMISE OF THE FINAL REDEMPTION

22:17 Because you performed this act . . . I will surely bless you and I will increase your offspring like the stars of the sky and the sand on the seashore and your offspring will conquer their enemies' gate—G-d had made the same promise previously,[91] stating that he would increase his offspring like the stars of heaven and the dust of the earth. But now G-d gave him additional assurance, swearing by His Great Name, that because he performed this great act, his offspring will conquer their enemies gate.

Avraham was now promised that no conceivable sin would bring about the destruction of his descendants, nor would they fall into the hands of their enemies and not rise again. Thus this is the ultimate promise of the redemption which is sure to come to us.

---

[91] *Bereishis* 13:16; 15:5.

תולדות

T O L E D O S

26:1 There was a famine in the land, aside from the first famine in the time of Avraham. Yitzchak went to Avimelech king of the Philistines in Gerar.

Aside from the first famine—Perhaps the Torah describes the famine in the days of Avrohom as the first famine because there was no famine in the world until Avraham's time.

In my opinion, the Torah is explaining that people of Yitzchak's era remembered that Avraham went down to Egypt because of the first famine, where G-d did him great honor. Yitzchak, following his father's example, planned to go to Egypt, but G-d told him, *Do not go down to Egypt* (26:2) "You are an unblemished offering[92]; it does not befit you to reside outside the Land".

A PORTENT FOR THE FUTURE

In my opinion, [Yitzchak's move to Gerar] signals events that would happen to his descendants in the future. Avraham's exile to Egypt because of the famine foreshadowed the exile of his descendants there. But his journey to Gerar[93] was not an exile, since he

---

[92] Since Yitzchak was brought on the altar as a sacrifice, he became sanctified like an offering.

[93] *Bereishis* ch.20.

moved there by choice. However Yitzchak was forced to Gerar from famine, therefore it portends a future exile. Yitzchak was exiled from his own place to the land of the Philistines, where his father had previously resided, foreshadowing the Babylonian exile, which was to a place that their ancestors had once resided, in Ur Kasdim. Furthermore, the events during the Babylonian exile parallel events that happened to Yitzchak in Gerar. Although Yitzchak suffered exile and fear in Gerar, they did not take his wife [as they did to Avraham in Egypt]. At first, Avimelech [king of Gerar] said, *Whoever touches this man or his wife shall die* (26:11). Later he regretted it, telling Yitzchak, *Go away from us* (26:16). Afterwards, he changed his mind once more and made a covenant with Yitzchak (26:25-31).

The Babylonian exile was similiar, they were exiled there because of famine, but they were neither enslaved nor treated badly. On the contrary, their leaders were appointed to high office in the Babylonian government, which later decreed, *Whoever is among you of His entire people—may his G-d be with him—and let him go up [to Eretz Yisrael]* (*Ezra* 1:3), instructing ministers of the province Beyond the River (Mesopotamia) [to be helpful to the Jews].[94] Afterwards they halted work [on the Beis Hamikdash] for a period of time, [corresponding to the cooling of Avimelech's friendship with Yitzchak, when he said, "Go away from us."] Changing their policy yet again, they gave permission to resume construction of the Beis Hamikdash, saying, *That they may offer pleasing sacrifices to the G-d of Heaven and pray for the life of the king and his sons* (*Ezra* 6:10) [corresponding to Avimelech making a covenant with Yitzchak.]

A NEW OATH TO YITZCHAK

26:3 I will fulfill the oath that I made to your father Avraham—This was not a promise to fulfill this oath, for it is inconceivable that G-d would not keep His word, for He is

---

94 *Nechemiah* 2:7-10.

not a human that He should change His mind. Nor did Avraham have other offspring on whom the covenant could be fulfilled except Yitzchak.[95] Nor was the oath given on condition; [that one might interpret that G-d was now saying that he will indeed fulfill the oath]. However in the case of Yaakov, because he had a brother Eisav, it was necessary that he be promised, *I will grant you the land that I gave to Avraham and Yitzchak* (35:12), to reassure him that the covenant will be fulfilled with him and not with Eisav.

It seems this phrase *I will keep the oath,* is in itself a [new] oath, [to Yitzchak]. Following this interpretation we can understand why the Torah says, *The land regarding which I made an oath to Avraham, Yitzchak and Yaakov* (*Devarim* 34:4), and, *Remember Your servants, Avraham, Yitzchak, and Yaakov. You swore to them by Yourself* (*Shemos* 32:13), for besides this verse, the Torah does not mention an oath to Yitzchak.

G-d swore to each of the Patriarchs individually, because each of the Patriarchs in his own right was worthy of the promise, and the merit of each one stands before Him to benefit their offspring. Even though the previous promise [to Avraham] was enough, as an additional merit and honor [the oath was repeated to each of them]. Therefore, G-d said, *I will remember my covenant with Yaakov as well as My covenant with Yitzchak and My covenant with Avraham, and I will remember the land* (*Vayikra* 26:42). He will remember that He made a covenant with each of them individually.

It is possible that with this oath, G-d swore additionally that He will grant Yitzchak the promise He had sworn to Avraham, to become a blessing to the nations, as He said to Avraham, *All the nations of the world will be blessed through your descendants* (*Bereishis* 22:18). Thus the meaning of the present verse is: [G-d says to Yitzchak:] Through you *I will fulfill the oath that I made to your father Avraham,* since you will be a blessing among the nations. The same way, G-d said to Yaakov, *All the families on earth will be blessed through you and your descendants* (28:14).

---

95 G-d specifically mentioned Yitzchok in the oath therefore Yishmael was not included.

FOUR CATEGORIES OF MITZVOS

26:5 All this is because Avraham obeyed My voice, and observed My safeguards, My commandments, My decrees, and My laws.

[Avraham] observed My safeguards—*Rashi* explains: "He obeyed My voice—when I tested him."

My safeguards, refer to Rabbinic enactments that serve as barriers against violation of Torah prohibitions, such as second degrees of forbidden marriages and Rabbinical prohibitions regarding Shabbos.

My commandments, refers to laws that man's moral sense would dictate, such as robbery and murder.

My decrees, refers to laws that reason cannot explain, such as the prohibition of eating swine and wearing garments woven of a mixture of wool and linen. These are royal decrees which G-d enacts on His subject.

and My laws, in the plural, are the Written Torah and the Oral Torah. The latter includes rules and interpretations transmitted to Moshe at Sinai. [End of *Rashi*'s commentary].

THE PATRIARCHS KEPT THE TORAH

According to this interpretation, Avraham observed the Torah although it was not yet given. The Sages indeed comment on the verse, *And Yosef gave [his brothers] wagons* (*Bereishis* 45:21),[96] that Yosef [hinted to his father that he was alive] because when he separated from him they were studying the chapter of "the calf

---

[96] The Hebrew word for wagons is *agalos* which can be translated also as "calves." By sending wagons to his father, Yosef hinted to the law of "the calf whose neck was broken" (*Devarim* 21:6), which he studied with his father before he was sold and taken to Egypt. He thereby signaled to his father that he was still alive.

whose neck was broken" (*Devarim* 21:1-9). Yaakov learned Torah just as his father and grandfather did, though the Torah had not yet been given. Indeed, when G-d says, *[Avraham] observed My safeguards, My commandments, My decrees, and My laws,* the Sages comment that Avraham observed the fine points of the law teaching them to his children.

A FUNDAMENTAL QUESTION

If [the Patriarchs observed the Torah before it was given,] why did Yaakov set up a pillar;[97] and why did he marry two sisters in their lifetime;[98] or in the opinion of our Sages, four sisters?[99] Why did Amram [Moshe's father] marry his aunt,[100] and Moshe, our teacher erect twelve pillars?[101] After all, G-d granted Avraham reward because he prohibited to himself what the Torah forbids, and furthermore he commanded his children and his household to follow in his ways?

The Sages taught that Yaakov observed Shabbos and set up Shabbos boundaries, [proving that Yaakov observed the Torah and emphasizing the apparent contradiction in setting up a pillar and marrying two sisters.] Perhaps Yaakov [only] observed Shabbos because it is as important as the entire Torah since it is testimony to G-d's creation of the world.

AVRAHAM OBSERVED THE SEVEN
NOACHIDE COMMANDMENTS

Perhaps the phrase *Avraham observed My safeguards* [which the Sages say comes to include second degree relatives] refers only

---

97 *Bereishis* 28:18; which is forbidden in *Devarim* 21:6.
98 Forbidden in *Vayikra* 18:18.
99 Bilhah and Zilpah were daughters of Lavan as were Rachel and Leah (*Bereishis Rabbah* 74:11).
100 *Shemos* 6:20. This is forbidden in *Vayikra* 12:13,14.
101 *Shemos* 24:4.

to prohibited second degree relatives of marriages forbidden by Noachide law.[102] *My commandments* applies to robbery and murder; *My decrees* refers to the prohibition against eating a limb of an animal before it is killed, as well as breeding mixed kinds of cattle or grafting together different species of trees, and *My laws* refers to the requirement of establishing a judicial system and the prohibition against idol worship. These [are Noachide] laws, binding on all mankind. Avraham fulfilled the will of the Creator, observing even the minutiae of the [Noachide] commandments, as the Sages said: "The tractate of idol worship which our father Avraham had, consisted of four hundred chapters."

In the same vein, the Sages explain the verse, *That year, [Yitzchak] reaped a hundred times [as much as he sowed]* (*Bereishis* 26:12) to mean he measured the produce to compute how much to tithe. [Although by Noachide law they are not obligated in tithes], the Patriarchs were generous men, giving tithes to the poor and to the priests of G-d, such as Shem and Ever and their students, as it says, *He was a priest to G-d, the Most High* (*Bereishis* 14:18).

It seems to me that the opinion of the Sages is, that Avraham knew the entire Torah through Divine inspiration and observed the mitzvos voluntarily, only in Eretz Yisrael. Yaakov married two sisters and Amram married his aunt when they were outside Eretz Yisrael. For the mitzvos are *the law of the G-d of the land* (2 *Melachim* 17:26), although we are required to keep personal mitzvos in every place. Our sages hinted at this idea [that the ful-

---

[102] The following are the seven Noachide laws which are binding on all mankind:
    (1) Do not murder.
    (2) Do not steal.
    (3) Do not worship false gods.
    (4) Do not be sexually immoral.
    (5) Do not eat the limb of an animal before it is killed.
    (6) Do not curse G-d.
    (7) Set up courts and bring offenders to justice.

fillment of Mitzvos in Eretz Yisroel has special significance] and I will expound[103] on it with the help of G-d.

The prohibition against erecting pillars was only introduced at a certain point in time [when Canaanites set up pillars for their idolatrous worship]. The Sages expound on the verse, *Do not erect a sacred pillar, since this is something Hashem, your G-d hates* (*Devarim* 16:27)—although [erecting a pillar] was pleasing to Him in the days of the Patriarchs, now He hates it, because the Canaanites used it for their idol worship.

According to the Rabbis, Yosef observed Shabbos even in Egypt [although it is outside Eretz Yisrael], because Shabbos is equal in importance to all the mitzvos, since it is testifies that G-d created the world out of nothing. He observed the Shabbos teaching his children to believe in the creation of the world and to reject the false doctrines and idolatry of the Egyptians. This is what the Sages had in mind [when they said the Patriarchs observed the Torah before it was given].

THE PLAIN MEANING OF THE VERSE

The plain meaning of our verse is as follows: *My safeguards* means Avraham believed in the Oneness of Hashem, safeguarding this in his heart, repudiating idol worship, calling out G-d's name and drawing many to His worship. *My commandments* means Avraham did all that G-d commanded him, such as: *Go away from your land* (12:1), bring your son as a burnt-offering, and drive out the maidservant (Hagar) and her son. *My decrees* implies that he walked in the path of G-d being gracious and compassionate, doing righteousness and justice, and commanding his children and household [to do] these things. *My laws* refers to the fact that Avraham circumcised himself, his sons and servants, and kept all the Noachide commandments which are their Torah.

---

[103] *Devarim* (11:18)

ALLUSION TO THE THREE BATEI MIKDASH

26:19-22 The servants of Yitzchak dug in the valley and there they found a well of living water. The shepherds of Gerar disputed with Isaac's shepherds, claiming the water was theirs. [Yitzchak] named the well *Eisek* (Quarreling), because they had challenged him. They dug another well and they disputed about it too, and he named it "Sitnah" (Hatred) . . . and they dug another well and they did not dispute over it, he named it "Rechovos" (Wide Spaces) saying now Hashem has expanded for us and we will be fruitful in the land.

He named the well *Eisek* (Quarreling)—The Torah speaks at length about the wells, although the story seemingly does not add to Yitzchak's reputation and honor. [Neither does it tell us anything new,] since both he and his father did the same thing.[104] However, the story of the wells, foretells the future.

A well of living water (26:19) alludes to the Beis Hamikdash which the descendants of Yitzchak will build. The Torah calls it *a well of living water*, just as it says, *Hashem, the source of living water* (*Yirmeyah* 17:13).[105]

He called the first well *Eisek* (Quarreling), alluding to the First Beis Hamikdash. The nations quarreled with us and made war against us over it, until they destroyed it.

He called the second well *Sitnah* (Hatred) (26:21), a harsher name than Quarreling. This refers to the Second Beis Hamikdash which has indeed been referred to by this very name (*Sitnah*) in the passage, *During the reign of Achashverosh, at the beginning of his reign, they wrote* sitnah *(hatred) against the inhabitants of Yehudah and Yerushalayim* (*Ezra* 4:6). Throughout its existence the nations

---

104 Both Avraham and Yitzchak dug wells in the land of the Philistines (*Bereishis* 21:30,31).

105 Thus, "a well of living water" alludes to the House of Hashem, the Beis Hamikdash.

hated us until they destroyed the Beis Hamikdash and sent us into bitter exile.

The third well which he called *Rechovos* (Wide Spaces) hints to the Third Beis Hamikdash which will be built speedily in our days, without quarreling and animosity. In its days G-d will expand our borders, as it says, *Hashem your G-d will [eventually] enlarge your borders, as He swore to your fathers* (*Devarim* 19:8). The Beis Hamikdash of the future is described as, *Broader [*rachavah*]*[106] *and spiraling upward* (*Yechezkel* 41:7). [The verse about the well *Rechovos* ends with,] *We will be fruitful in the land* (*Bereishis* 26:22), an indication that all nations will come to worship G-d with one voice.

THE NAME BEERSHEVA

26:32
On that very day, Yitzchak's servants came and told him about the well they had been digging. "We have found water!" they announced.

[They] told him about the well they had been digging—This is the well mentioned above, *His servants dug a well in the area* (26:25). [When he came to Beersheva] they began to dig it, and while they were digging, Avimelech and his company came. They made a covenant with Yitzchak, and left, after which Yitzchak's servants announced that they had found water.

[The name Beersheva commemorates two occurrences: the *be'er* (well) and the *shevuah* (oath)]. Is seems to me that this is the well Avraham dug, giving Avimelech seven lambs as a witness [that he owned it].[107] The Philistines plugged up this and other wells, whereupon Yitzchak dug it up again and called it *Shiv'ah*, the same name his father had called it. The city is called Beersheva, since this

---

106 from *rachav*, the same root as *Rechovos*.
107 *Bereishis* 21:30.

well (*be'er*), was named *shevuah* (oath) by both father and son, for there the two of them took an oath.[108]

This well alludes to the *Mishkan* in Shiloh. The Philistines plugged it up hinting to the Philistines taking away the Ark [from the *Mishkan* in Shiloh] (1 *Shmuel* 4:11). The redigging of the well indicates the Philistines returning the Ark along with a gift to G-d (6:11).

---

[108] Avraham swore in 21:30; Yitzchak in 26:31.

ויצא

VAYEITZEI

YAAKOV'S VISION

28:12 [Yaakov] had a vision in a dream. A ladder was standing on the ground, and its top reached upward toward heaven. G-d's angels were going up and down on it.

[Yaakov] had a vision in a dream—G-d showed him in a prophetic dream that everything on earth is accomplished through angels, who fulfill the decree G-d gives them. G-d sends angels to roam the earth who do not lift a finger until they return before the Master of the earth, telling Him: "We have wandered about the earth, and we report that all is at peace," or, "that it is bathed in blood and battle." G-d then commands them to return to earth and carry out His orders.

By showing Yaakov that He stands above the ladder, G-d gave His solemn assurance that his destiny will not be controlled by angels. Rather, he will be G-d's portion, and G-d will be with him always. This is a loftier level than other righteous people about whom it says, *He will order His angels to guard you wherever you go* (*Tehillim* 91:11).

WHY DID THE ANGELS GO UP AND DOWN?

In the view of Rabbi Eliezer Hagadol, Yaakov's vision was similar to the vision Avraham had at the Pact Between Halves[109] where he was shown the rise and fall of the Four Kingdoms.[110] Therefore the name for G-d in this verse is *Elohim* [the name associated with judgement]. This dream thus, is similar to the vision of Daniel where he saw the guardian angels of the kingdoms of Greece and Persia. G-d also promised Yaakov that He will be with him wherever he will go among the nations, guarding and rescuing him from them.

Thus Rabbi Eliezer Hagadol said: "The Holy One, blessed be He, showed Yaakov the rise and fall of the Four Kingdoms. He showed him the guardian angel of the kingdom of Babylonia rising and descending seventy rungs [representing the seventy years of Babylonian exile]. Then He showed him the guardian angel of the kingdom of Media (Persia) rising and descending 52 rungs. Next, the guardian angel of the kingdom of Greece rose and descended 180 rungs. Yaakov saw the guardian angel of the kingdom of Edom (Rome) rising but not descending, [because the *galus* of Edom (Rome) continues to this day].

ALLUSIONS TO THE BEIS HAMIKDASH

29:2 [Yaakov came to a place] where he saw a well in the field. Three herds of sheep were lying beside it, since it was from this well that the flocks were watered. The top of the well was covered with a large stone.

He saw a well in the field. Three flocks of sheep were lying beside it—The Torah elaborates here to teach us that those whose hope is in Hashem will have renewed strength, and the fear of G-d

---

[109] *Bereishis* 15:19-18.

[110] The four powers that ruled the ancient world and dominated Yisrael: Babylonia, Persia, Greece, and Rome. Our present-day *galus* is the continuing *galus* of Rome.

gives strength. Thus our father Yaakov arrived tired from a long trip, yet he rolled away the stone alone, a feat that took the combined strength of all the shepherds. The shepherds of the three herds lying beside the well could not budge it.

Our Rabbis in *Bereishis Rabbah* 70:8, explain this verse prophetically. Yaakov entered Charan by way of the well, when only three of all the herds were gathered, the stone was still lying on the well, and the flocks were waiting [to be watered]. These details showed Yaakov that he would be successful in his undertaking, and will have children who will see the fulfillment of the things alluded to [in this verse]. The well alludes to the Beis Hamikdash, and the three flocks of sheep hint to the pilgrims going to Yerushalayim for the three Yamim Tovim.[111] The phrase, *since it was from this well that the flocks were watered*, means the pilgrims were inspired from the Beis Hamikdash. Alternatively, the verse [about watering the flocks] alludes to the Torah, for it says, *For from Zion the Torah will come forth, and the word of Hashem from Yerushalayim* (*Yeshayah* 2:3), and the Torah is compared to water.

The next verse, *When all the flocks would come together there* (29:3), alludes to [the inauguration of the Beis Hamikdash by Shlomoh, which was followed by the Yom Tov of Sukkos celebrated by] *a huge congregation, [extending] from the Approach of Chamas until the Brook of Egypt* (1 *Melachim* 8:65).

[The shepherds] would roll the stone from the top of the well and water the sheep, because the pilgrims drew holy inspiration from there. *Then they would replace the stone on the well*, to lie inactive until the following Yom Tov.

RACHEL'S REQUEST

30:1,2 Rachel realized that she was not bearing any children to Yaakov . . . She said to Yaakov, "Give

---

[111] Pesach, Shavuos, and Sukkos.

me children! If not, let me die!" Yaakov got angry at Rachel saying, "Shall I take G-d's place who withheld children from you".

Give me children!—The commentators say she meant to ask Yaakov to pray for her.

"If not, let me die!"—Rashi comments: One who has no children is considered dead.[112]

But I wonder about this interpretation. If she asked him to pray for her, why did he become furious saying, *Shall I take G-d's place?* (30:2). After all, G-d listens to the payers of the righteous. I wonder also that Yaakov said, [to Rachel, as stated in Rashi: "You ask that I do like my father, who prayed for Rivkah to have children. I am not in the same situation as my father.] My father had no sons [when he prayed], but I do have sons. It is from you that G-d has withheld [children], not from me." Don't the righteous pray for others? Surely Eliyahu and Elisha prayed on behalf of strange women.

It seems that our Rabbis [bothered by these questions] criticized Yaakov, saying: The Holy One, blessed be He, said to Yaakov, "Is this the way you answer a woman who is heartsick [because she has no children]? I swear that your children will stand [contrite] before her son [Yosef]!"

The simple way to understand this dialogue is that Rachel demanded that Yaakov give her children, intending that he keep praying until G-d granted her children, threatening to die of despair otherwise. In her envy [of her sister] she spoke in an unbefitting way,[113] thinking that since Yaakov loved her he would fast, dress in sackcloth and ashes, and pray until she had children, so she should not die of her misery.

---

[112] *Bereishis Rabbah* 71:9.

[113] She should have accepted her distress with love, believing that it is all for the best. She should have prayed and hoped that G-d will have mercy on her. She should not have despaired and mentioned dying (*P'nei Yerushalayim*).

WHY YAAKOV BECAME ANGRY

Yaakov became furious because the righteous do not have the power to have all their prayers answered. Because she implored him, appealing to his love, and threatening him with her death, he became angry with her, telling her that he could not take the place of G-d, Who grants children to barren women. He said, G-d withheld children from her, not from him, to admonish and shame her [for the way she had spoken]. When the righteous Rachel saw that she could not rely on Yaakov's prayer, she herself decided to pray to G-d, Who listens to those who cry out to Him. And so, *G-d heard her prayer and opened her womb* (30:22).

Perhaps we can justify the commentary of the Rabbis of the Midrash [who say Yaakov told Rachel: "It is from you that G-d has withheld children, not from me."] Surely Yaakov prayed for his beloved wife who was childless, but his prayer was not accepted. However, Rachel pressured Yaakov to continue to pray that she have children anyway, telling him that he was no less [pious] than his father, who [prayed for Rivkah and was answered]. Her badgering made him angry. He told her that the matter was in G-d's hand, not his, and his father's prayer had been answered [not because of his insistence, but] because of his righteousness and because he was destined to have children. However, in her case, G-d [for his reasons] kept her from having children. This is what the Sages had in mind.

GLOSSARY

———◦◉◦———

AGGADA - Homiletic discourses
AVRAHAM AVINU - Abraham our Father
B'NEI YISRAEL - Children of Israel
BAMIDBAR - The Book of Numbers
BEIS HAMIKDASH - Holy Temple
BEREISHIS - The Book of Genesis
CHAVAKUK - Habakuk
DEVARIM - The Book of Deuteronomy
DIVREI HAYAMIM - The Book of Chronicles
EICHA - The Book of Lamentations
ELOHIM - God
ERETZ YISRAEL - The Land of Israel
HASHEM - God
HASHGACHAH - Divine Providence
HOSHEA - The Book of Hosea
IYOV - Job
KOHEN pl. *KOHANIM* - Priests, descendants of Aaron
KOHELES - Ecclesiastes
LEVITES - from the tribe of Levi
MASHIACH - The Messiah
MELACHIM - The Book of Kings
MILAH - circumcision
MISHKAN - The Tabernacle
MISHLEI - Proverbs
MITZVAH pl. *MITZVOS* - commandment
MOSHE RABBEINU - Moses our Teacher

NIDDAH - menstruant woman
NOACH - Noah
ONKELOS - A convert who wrote an Aramaic translation of the
    Torah
PARASHA - the portion [of the Torah]
SANHEDRIN - Jewish High Court
SEFER - book or scroll
SHABBOS - The day of rest - Saturday
SHAVUOS - Festival of Weeks
SHECHINA - Divine Presence
SHEMOS - The Book of Exodus
SHIR HASHIRIM - Song of Songs
SHLOMOH - Solomon
SHMUEL - The Book of Samuel
SHOFTIM - The Book of Judges
SUKKOS - Festival of Tabernacles
TANACH - Scriptures
TEHILLIM - Psalms
TERUMAH pl. *TERUMOS* - contribution to the Kohein
TZADDIK - Pious Person
VAYIKRA - The Book of Leviticus
YAAKOV - Jacob
YAMIM TOVIM - holidays
YECHEZKEL - Ezekiel
YEHOSHUA - Joshua
YERUSHALAYIM - Jerusalem
YESHAYAH - Isaiah
YIRMIYAH - Jeremiah
YISRAEL - Israel
YITZCHOCK - Isaac
YOEL - Joel